T0207758

Endorsements

As a pastor, I have seen the sacred trust of couples broken in more marriages than I can count. Many times I've sought to help couples through a devastating breach of trust, only to struggle to find the pathway to healing. Finally, Ellen Dean has produced a resource that will provide the guidance many of us have been seeking. Not only does she bring a deep biblical understanding of what it takes to see the redemptive work of God when trust is broken, she also provides a clear pathway toward healing and restoration. I know of no other resource like this. Thank you, Ellen, for this great gift to us all!

Dr. Jeff Warren
Senior Pastor, Park Cities Baptist Church, Dallas, Texas

I am so grateful for this much needed guide that addresses this most painful of issues. Whether you are seeking to rebuild your marriage, doubting whether trust can be re-established or, like me, want to help couples who bring these painful stories my way, Marriage Trust Builders provides a biblical and realistic path for restoration and hope. I highly recommend it.

Jack Graham
Pastor, Prestonwood Baptist Church, Dallas, Texas

In today's society, many marriages are struggling. A key component in many of the struggles is an erosion of trust. In her book, <u>Marriage Trust Builders</u>, Ellen Dean has captured the heart of trust issues in a marital relationship. She has provided a helpful resource to help build trust and companionship in marital relationships. Although there are many books on marriage, there is a lack of resources to lead a married couple on a journey of healing. Ellen has provided such a resource in this wonderful book. She goes directly to the heart of any marriage, which is the spiritual component. <u>Marriage Trust Builders</u> deals with pertinent Biblical passages which outline principles of restoration. The work is broken into three sections which helps the reader discover trust issues, begin the rebuilding process, and become aware of marital trigger points. Dean discusses vital topics in marriages, such as trust erosion, confession of sin, and self-awareness. The book is strengthened by case studies from Dean's many years of practice in Biblical counseling and self-reflective questions for both spouses. Overall, this book is a practical, Biblically-sound resource for any marriage to build trust and thrive.

Dr. Greg Ammons,
Senior Pastor, First Baptist Church, Garland, Texas

I have known Ellen Dean for the last thirty years, and I admire and respect her ministry of counseling. This book will serve as a great resource to those who desire a Christian approach for healing and restoration of a weak or broken marriage. Ellen provides hope that with the Lord's help, indeed healing and restoration can take place.

Gary Cook
Chancellor, Dallas Baptist University

There is not a more practical subject to address than marriage. I like how Ellen addresses the subject of marital trust in such a tender way. You will find hope on every page, as well as practical next steps for those seeking to restore, or help others restore their marriage.

Dr. Mark Dance
Director- LifeWay Pastors

In her book, <u>Marriage Trust Builders</u>, Ellen Dean does a remarkable job of addressing the issue of rebuilding trust in a marriage when trust has been broken. She writes from years of experience as a biblical counselor, anchoring her work upon God's life transforming Word, in a spirit of gentleness and grace. The Lord is using this work to hold out hope to anyone or any marriage that is marred from broken trust. He is Faithful!

Steve Hardin
Campus Pastor, The Village Church, Dallas
Northway Campus, Dallas, Texas

I have been made aware and personally observed the positive results issuing out of the counseling ministry of Ellen Dean for years. The principles in this volume are not simply theoretical; they have been beaten out on the anvil of intense personal involvement with thousands of couples. This is a book with practical truths we can all "put a handle on" and productively apply to our own lives and marriages. Woven through the pages, sometimes subtly, sometimes more obviously, is One and only One who is known as our "Wonderful Counselor." Read it...and reap! After all, it is never too late for a new beginning!

O.S. Hawkins
President of Guidestone

Ellen Dean has provided an excellent resource for married couples to lead them through the journey of marital healing. Pathways that address heart issues, practical responsibilities and Biblical truth to discovering, rebuilding and restoring the foundation of trust that God desires in our marriages and our personal relationship with Him.

Neal Jeffrey
Associate Pastor, Minister of Pastoral Ministries,
Prestonwood Baptist Church, Dallas, Texas.

I highly recommend to you <u>Marriage Trust Builders</u> by my friend, Ellen Dean. In her years of counseling married couples, dealing with a variety of issues and challenges, she has gleaned a great deal of wisdom and insight into these delicate and damaging situations that happen in a marriage relationship. Anyone who has a good marriage knows that it comes about with a great deal of work and commitment. This book can be an excellent tool in helping married couples navigate these potentially crippling situations.

Chris Liebrum
Director, Office of Texas Baptists Cooperative Program
Ministry, Baptist General Convention of Texas

In a day when Christian marriages between a man and woman seem to fail, Ellen Dean points to critical strategies for couples to consider to build strong families. A healthy, strong, and enduring marriage is one of the best gifts parents can give to their children and grandchildren. Ellen's book will help you give that gift.

Albert L. Reyes, DMin, PhD
President and CEO, Buckner International, Dallas, Texas

Ellen Dean's prayer has been answered! She asked God for this book to give "comfort and direction" to those experiencing marriage challenges and both have been granted in <u>Marriage Trust Builders</u>. Her insights on trust as a critical component for healthy marriages are wise, engaging, practical, doable and grounded. Because this work gets to the heart of the matter in marriage while giving honest assessments laced with hope, her book will be a welcomed resource to share with people in my own pastoral ministry for years to come.

Dr. David Rogers
Lead Pastor, Arapaho Road Baptist Church, Garland, Texas

I've been blessed by Ellen Dean's biblical counseling ministry, both for our family and as my primary source for referrals for our church family, for years. Her writing on restoring trust in marriage will serve as a resource for me as a pastor and a tool for use in ministry with couples. It captures what I appreciate about Ellen's ministry. It's practical, grace-filled, and uncompromisingly biblical.

Chad Selph
Senior Pastor, First Baptist Church, Allen, Texas

As a pastor, a great part of my counseling sessions are spent addressing family issues and concerns. Spouses who committed themselves in martial vows sometimes find out that the fairy tale of living "happily ever after" is often more challenging then they could have ever imagined. Misconceptions, broken trust, false expectations and all contribute to couples that were once happy end up hating and despising one another with a passion. By the time many of these couples enter my office, a great deal of damage in the marriage has already been done. And I am now in a position as the last ditch effort to help them put the shattered pieces of the once fairy tale turned horror story into something salvageable.

As I sit and hear from both sides through their arguments, harsh words, disappointments and anger, and try to make sense of the madness before me, I know that my task is to walk with these couples to make the best of a devastating situation. The book, Marriage Trust Builders, is a tool that can be used in various counseling sessions to assist couples in working through the hurt and pain to restore broken relationships. What this book presents is a biblical approach to helping couples see how God desires for them to work through their marriage crises and begin the rebuilding phase.

The book also is not only filled with biblical passages that help the counselor and the couple think about what God desires in marriage, but the practical stories and examples to help families understand that they are not the only ones facing challenges in marriage. The hope that the book brings out is that marriages can be rebuilt and love can be reestablished through hard work and commitment.

After reading parts of this work, I would suggest that every pastor read this book to help develop a framework in their marriage counseling sessions and also consider using the book in marriage seminars and retreats to help strengthen marriages within the church.

Chris Simmons
Pastor of Cornerstone Baptist Church, Dallas, Texas

I highly recommend this book. I have known Ellen and her husband, Bob, for almost a decade. It has been my privilege to serve as their Pastor. I have seen them display everything that Ellen writes in her book. They love and serve each other with integrity and grace. Ellen writes not just from her head but from her heart. She communicates not just on a theoretical level, but on a very practical and experiential level. Ellen references countless situations that couples face. As you read her book, you will begin to think that she has been closely observing your marriage, and you will also be convinced that the counsel she shares won't just help your marriage, it will transform it.

Dr. Gary Singleton
Senior Pastor, The Heights Baptist Church, Richardson, Texas

Today, there are many books about marriage, but <u>Marriage Trust Builders</u> is unique. God has been using Ellen Dean for over 20 years to help hundreds of couples restore trust in their marriage. She uses a Biblical model of counseling which offers true hope and the power to change the lives of couples. Ellen and Bob Dean have been married over 40 years and have served in ministry together through these years.

Ellen has applied the insights that she has learned about the common obstacles and difficulties faced by couples with broken trust in writing this practical and Biblical guide. It is full of scripture and practical examples. It will be a help to any couple needing to strengthen the trust in their marriage. This book will be useful to pastors, counselors, and friends seeking to help struggling couples.

Dr. David W. Smith
Executive Director, Austin Baptist Association, Austin, Texas

In <u>Marriage Trust Builders</u>, Ellen Dean gives practical and essential guidance for the long and tough journey to reestablish the foundation of trust that every great marriage is built upon.

Steve Stroope
Lead Pastor, Lake Pointe Church, Rockwall, Texas

The process of healing from broken trust within a relationship is often messy, but with God as the author of your story, He can transform the situation into a beautiful mess. In this book, Ellen shares sage guidance on the process of restoring trust in a marriage while consistently and beautifully pointing the couple to Christ and His Word for ultimate healing of the relationship. Trust is a foundational element for any healthy marriage and this book will encourage and support couples toward building or rebuilding the bedrock of their marriage.

Katie Swafford M.A., L.P.C.-S., Ph.D. in Leadership, Director,
Texas Baptists Counseling Services Connections Team

As have many others, I have been sending folks to Ellen Dean for marital counseling for years. The reason is simple. I have complete confidence in her ability to help folks. Her new book Marriage Trust Builders offers more of the Biblical, straight shooting, practical help that we have come to expect from her. Read it, and share it with your folks! You won't be sorry! Thanks, Ellen!

Steve Swofford, Pastor
First Baptist Church, Rockwall, Texas

God's word does not return void, and Marriage Trust Builders does not disappoint. Saturated in the Scriptures and seasoned with wisdom, Ellen not only identifies pressing issues facing couples in every season, but graciously points to solutions to better every marriage. Her years of counseling and love of God has produced a work that is both excellent and sure to benefit the body of Christ to the glory of God and the joy of your soul.

Dr. Adam Wright,
President of Dallas Baptist University, Dallas, Texas

Marriage
Trust
Builders

A Practical and Biblical
Guide for Strengthening and
Restoring Trust in Marriage

For Those Who Are Hurting and Those Who are Helping

Ellen Dean

WESTBOW
PRESS®
A DIVISION OF THOMAS NELSON
& ZONDERVAN

This book is a work of non-fiction. Unless otherwise noted, the author and the publisher make no explicit guarantees as to the accuracy of the information contained in this book and in some cases, names of people and places have been altered to protect their privacy.

WestBow Press books may be ordered through booksellers or by contacting:

WestBow Press
A Division of Thomas Nelson & Zondervan
1663 Liberty Drive
Bloomington, IN 47403
www.westbowpress.com
1 (866) 928-1240

Because of the dynamic nature of the Internet, any web addresses or links contained in this book may have changed since publication and may no longer be valid. The views expressed in this work are solely those of the author and do not necessarily reflect the views of the publisher, and the publisher hereby disclaims any responsibility for them.

Any people depicted in stock imagery provided by Getty Images are models, and such images are being used for illustrative purposes only. Certain stock imagery © Getty Images.

THE HOLY BIBLE, NEW INTERNATIONAL VERSION®, NIV® Copyright © 1973, 1978, 1984, 2011 by Biblica, Inc.® Used by permission. All rights reserved worldwide.

All italics in scripture quotations represent author's added emphasis.

ISBN: 978-1-9736-2881-1 (sc)
ISBN: 978-1-9736-2880-4 (hc)
ISBN: 978-1-9736-2879-8 (e)

Library of Congress Control Number: 2018905927

Print information available on the last page.

WestBow Press rev. date: 5/22/2018

Dedication

This book is dedicated to my precious husband, Bob
Dean, for his many hours of listening, reading, editing,
and praying with me as I completed this book. His endless
encouragement and unconditional love are amazing
blessings in my life. He is truly the most loving, patient,
trustworthy, and Christlike person I have ever known.

Bob, I love you with all my heart.

Contents

Introduction xv

Part 1 – Discovery

Chapter 1   Becoming Aware. 1

Chapter 2   First Steps 11

Chapter 3   Caught and Confronted 19

Chapter 4   Heart Conviction That Leads to Confession 27

Chapter 5   Disclosure 39

Part 2 – Rebuilding

Chapter 6   Confession 55

Chapter 7   Severing Wrong Relationships 67

Chapter 8   Repentance and Heart Issues 83

Chapter 9   Understanding the Emotions and Responses 95

Chapter 10 Forgiveness 117

Part 3 – Restoration

Chapter 11 Triggers and Temptations 135

Chapter 12 Accountability 153

Chapter 13 Protecting Your Marriage 167

Chapter 14 Investing in Your Marriage 187

Chapter 15 The Importance of Trust 207

Endnotes 221

Introduction

Most adults know someone who has experienced the pain and suffering resulting from marital trust being broken. Perhaps that someone is you, a member of your family, a friend, an acquaintance, or someone you have chosen to encourage and assist in some way as a result of broken trust in a marriage. Sadly, the problem is common and widespread.

When trust is broken in a marriage, it produces a unique set of emotions and factors that need to be addressed carefully and compassionately. It involves heartache on both sides and impacts many other people. It has far-reaching effects and long-lasting results. All these aspects need to be considered in the plan for care and growth.

In my counseling practice I see many marriages. Situations involving broken trust probably encompass more than half of them. Through the years, that has added up to hundreds of couples that I have worked with. The large majority of these couples have experienced healing and a renewed marriage because of God's Word, His love, and His grace. The couples were willing to apply biblical instructions for restoration.

In working with these couples, I have not been able to find a resource that thoroughly engages couples and leads them through the journey of healing. The resources that I do know about often do not adequately address the heart issues, the practical matters, or the related biblical truths.

Needing a resource has resulted in my decision to write this book. This is not a perfect book, just as my counseling is not perfect. However, God is perfect, and He is the Wonderful Counselor. He loves every hurting person and marriage. The Bible is very relevant and practical. It provides the plan and solutions.

This book is divided into three parts. Part 1 deals with the discovery of broken trust and the emotional devastation that results. It explains taking the initial right actions, disclosing facts, confronting the offender, and listening to the Holy Spirit.

Part 2 begins the rebuilding process. It involves confession, how to sever wrong relationships, recognizing the heart issues, moving toward repentance, understanding the emotions of both spouses, and explaining the why and how of forgiveness.

Part 3 discusses the importance of being aware of triggers and temptations and how to stand strong against them. It also includes how to develop accountability, how to protect the marriage, and how to invest meaningfully in the marriage. The importance of trust is explained, and several specific avenues of application are addressed.

In referring to the spouse who has caused the breach of trust, I have used the terms *unfaithful spouse* and *offending spouse*. For the spouse whose trust was broken I used the terms *faithful spouse*, *offended spouse*, and *hurting spouse*. These terms are relating to the specific reasons and incidents that have hurt the spouse and the marriage. This does not imply unfaithfulness in all areas of life or faithfulness in all areas of life. The truth is that everyone is a sinner and sins at times. Everyone needs Jesus Christ as Savior and the forgiveness He offers.

Questions to Ask Regarding the Trust in Your Marriage

Below are some questions regarding trust in marriage. These can be used to assess and target areas for improvement. Each spouse can consider these questions personally and pertaining to his or her spouse. The questions can spark desire for growth and new direction in the marriage. The marriage deserves every effort to strengthen the commitment and trust.

Some Questions to Ask Regarding Yourself

- Do I live in a way that honors God and act with integrity and purity? Do I have a strong moral compass?
- Do I care about the needs and interests of my spouse and family?
- Do I follow through on agreements, commitments, and responsibilities?
- Do I control my emotions appropriately?
- Do my actions show my spouse that I want to be trustworthy in everything?

Some Questions to Ask Regarding Your Spouse

- Does my spouse live in a way that honors God and act with integrity and purity? Does my spouse have a strong moral compass?
- Does my spouse care about my needs and interests and those of our family?
- Does my spouse follow through on agreements, commitments, and responsibilities?
- Does my spouse control emotions appropriately?
- Do my spouse's actions show me that he or she wants to be trustworthy in everything?

Think about these questions carefully. If the trust in your relationship is weak or broken, please continue to read this book with a commitment to seek to improve the trust. Don't settle for a mediocre marriage when you can have a great marriage.

Sometimes the trust is not just weak but has been shattered in marriages. In these cases couples need hope and loving support. They also need understanding and guidance in processing emotions and decisions. Those topics will be discussed in this book. Hopefully, the information will be beneficial to spouses and to helpers.

There are many ways that trust can be broken in marriage. One area that this book does not address is that of domestic abuse. It is not ever acceptable for there to be abuse of any kind in a marriage or family. Abuse is control over vulnerable or weaker individuals. When abuse is present, the family members who are being victimized should seek help and safety for themselves and other family members. Abuse issues should not be minimized or overlooked.

My prayer is that this book will give comfort and direction to those who are hurting, to those who have caused the pain, and to those who are assisting and walking alongside. I long for this book to point people to Jesus Christ for salvation, comfort, strength, guidance, and healing. I pray that God will be glorified through this book.

Part 1 – Discovery

Chapter 1 – Becoming Aware

This chapter shows some examples of how a spouse may learn that the trust has been broken in the marriage. It discusses the emotions felt and how these issues need to be addressed. It provides hope and comfort.

Chapter 2 – First Steps

It is important to know what to do when trust has been broken in a marriage. This requires wisdom and foresight to intentionally implement an effective plan regarding what will be beneficial with appropriate actions.

Chapter 3 – Caught and Confrontation

This explains how to confront a spouse who has been caught in actions that break the trust in the marriage. Purpose is explained, guidance is given, and cautions are discussed in the process of confrontation.

Chapter 4 – Disclosure

Disclosure describes how facts come to light in many ways and from different sources. It stresses the need for all the facts to be revealed in order to rebuild trust. Disclosure is different than confession.

Chapter 5 – Heart Conviction that Leads to Confession

Sometimes a spouse was unfaithful earlier in the marriage and now is feeling the conviction to confess. It is important to know what to do and how to handle that confession.

Part 2 – Rebuilding

Chapter 6 – Confession

Confession is the humble, honest acknowledgment of sins committed. It includes accepting responsibility of personal wrongs and choosing to ask for forgiveness and seek restoration.

Chapter 7 – Severing Wrong Relationships

Wrong relationships need to be thoroughly severed before a couple can begin to move forward after trust has been broken. Appropriately severing a relationship is crucial in order to begin rebuilding the confidence in the marriage.

Chapter 8 – Repentance and Heart Issues

Repentance means changing from bad actions and attitudes to replacing them with a new understanding of holiness and trustworthiness. There are many heart issues that are involved in repentance and the commitment to change.

Chapter 9 – Understanding the Emotions and Responses

Broken trust in marriage brings a plethora of emotions for both spouses. Understanding the spectrum of emotions and providing tools to help process them are keys for healing the pain of broken trust.

Chapter 10 – Forgiveness

Forgiveness is letting go of the hurt caused by the sinful actions of others. It involves understanding God's grace and the forgiveness that He offers to us. Then we respond with faith to offer forgiveness to others.

Part 3 – Restoration

Chapter 11 – Triggers and Temptations

Triggers spark past interests, and temptations lure into sinful actions. Crucial awareness and strong decisions are needed to prevent further harm, which can follow from giving in to temptations because of a lack of self-control.

Chapter 12 – Accountability

Accountability is the transparency of all information between spouses. It is involved in all areas of life. It establishes proof of personal integrity. Accountability builds trustworthiness and eliminates secrecy between spouses.

Chapter 13 – Protecting the Marriage

Protecting marriage means making strong pledges regarding how to act toward all other people of the opposite gender outside the marriage. Protecting marriage involves boundaries, discretion, and commitments.

Chapter 14 – Investing in Your Marriage

Investing in your marriage regularly in loving ways helps to preserve it as a special treasure. Expressing appreciation daily, giving quality time, and celebrating special moments and events show that you value your spouse.

Chapter 15 – The Importance of Trust

God wants marriages to be filled with trust. Trust is foundational to a strong and healthy marriage. Confidence in one's spouse brings love and joy to the marriage. Truthfulness and dependability provide the assurance that marriages need and deserve.

Part 1

Discovery

1

Becoming Aware

But it is you, ... my companion, my close friend
with whom I once enjoyed sweet fellowship.
—Psalm 55:13–14

You thought nothing like this could ever happen to you. You married for life. This was not what you planned or ever anticipated. It's as if your world has been turned upside down. The trust has been broken and the commitment completely disrupted in your marriage. Things have been shaken to the core.

There are many scenarios in which a marriage can enter an emergency time that causes a trust crisis in the marriage. It may result from financial actions, irresponsibility, impulsivity, sexual sins, unfaithfulness, or many other reasons. These examples may sound familiar and close to home. Perhaps one of these sounds similar to your story or that of someone you know and care about.

Ben and Jackie

Ben and Jackie are sitting in counseling, both talking at once and not listening to each other. Their anger is driving the conversation. Underneath is deep hurt. A few days ago, Jackie was looking at the bank statements and noticed that Ben had recently made some major purchases that he had not discussed with her. She looked further and realized that they were items she had never even seen.

Before Ben came home from work that evening, Jackie had planned carefully how to gather the needed information and explanations. However, soon after Ben arrived, the questions began to flow. Frustration and defensiveness took over. Nothing was resolved. Since then they have not been communicating except for the bare essentials.

Allen and Beth

Allen and Beth sit silent and distant while tears roll down her cheeks. After some initial questions, it is revealed that Beth has felt distant from Allen for months. She wonders why their relationship is changing from what characteristically has been open, fun, and caring. Allen has become aloof and self-focused. In the past, they have shared computers and passwords. Recently, Allen has changed his and is not willing to disclose them to Beth.

Early in the morning, Beth does some checking on the computer and finds tracks of Allen's pornographic searches. She remembers that recently Allen's showers and trips to the restroom have become longer and more frequent. When she confronts him, he acknowledges that a co-worker showed him some porn sites, and a past dormant interest has been revived.

Fred and Laura

Fred called for the appointment and asked Laura to come too. He tried several times before she finally agreed. Fred is somber and close to tears; Laura is fidgety and looks uncomfortable. The week before, Fred learned that Laura has been having an affair with a neighbor. The man's wife called Fred and told him about it.

Fred is the quiet type, and Laura is outgoing and talkative. She enjoys lots of affirmation and activity. Laura is very pretty and clearly uses her beauty to get the attention she expects. In the last few months, she has been argumentative whenever Fred asks her about her schedule or her whereabouts. She explains that she is not as much of a homebody as he is.

James and Heather

James and Heather were high school sweethearts and married right out of college. Recently, James took an out-of-town trip with his work. While he was away, Heather cleaned out the garage and their cars. Behind James's workbench she found some magazines and realized they were pornographic. When she looked in his car trunk, she saw some others stuffed partway under the carpet.

Heather called James and told him what she had found. James told her she was crazy and totally denied the magazines. He later changed his answer and told her that he was storing them for a friend at work. When he came home, Heather asked him to go to counseling. He agreed only when Heather threatened to leave and take the children away if he would not go to counseling with her.

Mark and Lindsey

Mark and Lindsey disagree and argue. Mark has been asking Lindsey why her conversations with him include inconsistencies and rationalizations. She is frequently caught in lies. When confronted about it, she tenaciously defends her stories. Whenever they make an agreement, Lindsey does the opposite of what they agreed. Later she denies any previous agreement.

Lindsey embellishes stories and says things to family and friends that Mark knows aren't true. He frequently questions her facts and explanations. Mark hears from other people things Lindsey says that he knows to be untrue. He is confused and frustrated by the lack of integrity in her speech and relationships.

Henry and Susan

Many people think Henry and Susan are the ideal couple. They are Christians, involved in church and active in their children's lives. They have good jobs and appear to be doing well. However, when they are honest, they admit to not being happy or confident about their marriage. Their trust is unsteady, and the emotional closeness is lacking.

Each one has privately wondered if this is as good as it gets for their relationship. Concerns weigh heavy on them as they go through life missing the joys of marriage that God intended. They wonder what could make things better.

Common Denominators

Common Experiences

As you were reading these examples, did it feel familiar, remind you of someone you know, break your heart for someone you love, or bring to light something hidden from past experiences? In these stories, did you see yourself, a friend, a family member, or perhaps someone else you have heard about?

All the names and scenarios of couples and persons mentioned in this book are fictitious. The stories are composites of common generic circumstances. Although ages, life stages, ethnic groups, and socioeconomic categories vary, they have one very significant similarity.

Trust Is Broken

The common denominator is that the trust is weak or has been broken in their marriage. Now their marriage is hurting and struggling. They need to know what to do next. The emotions in such situations are varied and usually extremely intense. The actions and decisions that the husband and wife make can greatly impact what happens to their marriage for a long time.

When trust is broken in a marriage, it is due to foregoing issues, circumstances, or events. Sometimes it is the result of several events or actions. Sometimes it is a pattern of disintegrating values and convictions. There are always emotional reactions that need to be measured and considerations that need to be discussed.

Repeating Characteristics

Usually the characteristics of the scenarios repeat similarly in different stories. It feels like a déjà vu with an eerie sensation of having been here many times before. Predictable precursors have compounded over time in these couples' lives, and it will require time and effort to sort things out and reach the best solutions and outcomes.

There are important goals and objectives, and these need careful and prayerful attention. In every situation, there are layers to the problems. The sins and needs are greater than one person or any human can solve alone. They are all complicated and sticky.

Intense Emotions

Though each couple is different and circumstances are unique, the emotions are probably very similar. When broken trust shatters a marriage, regardless of the precipitating factors, the intense emotions are hard to adequately describe. They range from shock, deep hurt, disbelief, discouragement, and anger to fear, guilt, confusion, betrayal, rejection, despair, disgust, and even panic.

The grief from broken trust in a marriage is one of the deepest hurts anyone can experience. Emotions are described in many ways: "It felt like a knife in my heart," "It was like being on a ship tossed at sea," "I felt like crying for days," "I've had the wind knocked out of me," and "I'm the last to know." A spouse may already feel battle-worn, overwhelmed, and emotionally weary by the time the facts begin to come out. You may be tempted to "make the other person pay" or to "throw in the towel"—to quit trying and end the marriage.

The flooding emotions are similar to feelings of deep grief and sorrow when a loved one dies tragically. It is very important for couples to know that the marriage has not died. Crucial decisions need to be made in a timely way. The lifeline needs to be thrown to these couples in the beginning as feelings, facts, and future decisions all collide.

If you are the partner who has just become aware that the trust you have had in your spouse and your marriage has been broken, then your emotions are probably indescribable and unfathomable. It seems as if your whole world has been turned upside down and shaken to the core. Deep hurt instantaneously wells up. The torrents of disbelief and heart-wrenching grief and the anguish of betrayal pour over you.

Perhaps you are feeling overwhelmed and so hurt you can hardly speak. It's hard to put one foot in front of another and function normally. You want to react and pull away all at the same time. Perhaps you feel numb and want to be far away from your spouse, or you may be continuing activities as if nothing has happened.

Often an initial response to hurtful actions is to lash back at the person who caused the pain. You want your spouse to understand how crushed you are, how deeply you are hurt, and how undeserving you are of the circumstances and the violation. You want an explanation and reasons. You want to know why and how. This is a confusing and dark time in a marriage.

All these emotions are valid and understandable. It is essential that you seek help with someone knowledgeable about what needs to happen now who can help you think clearly and act wisely. Be intentional to talk with a minister or a biblical counselor as soon as possible. There is light coming, and help is available.

In the midst of the emotional tumult, thoughts and feeling

are crashing. The circumstances can feel hopeless and the future completely a fog. Whatever you felt certain about earlier now probably seems to have vanished away. Fear or anger may grip you.

However, there are some important facts to remember. God is the Lord. His attributes remain true. His faithfulness is steadfast, His truth is perfect, His strength is unshakable, and His desire is for you to know Him and trust Him. God will never change or break your trust. Jesus Christ will give amazing comfort, strength, and wisdom as you seek Him. He is the Lord of lords and the King of kings for all eternity. Run to God. He will scoop you into His arms and say, "I will never leave you or forsake you."

> The LORD himself goes before you and will be with you; he will never leave you nor forsake you. Do not be afraid; do not be discouraged. (Deuteronomy 31:8)

The Most Important Things to Know

The most important consideration is to pursue God and His Word for wisdom, direction, clarity, growth, change, and forgiveness. He knows everything, loves everyone, and has a plan and a will that supersedes all else. God is our refuge, our Father, our Lord, our redeemer, our strength, our comfort, and our king, just to name a few. Go to Him. He will welcome you with open arms and guide each step as you follow Him.

God will help with disclosure; He teaches confession and acknowledgement. He increases our faith, encourages repentance, models forgiveness, and blesses from His incomparable riches. We can trust Him and rest in Him. Jesus Christ died for sin, including the sins that have wrecked your marriage. He wants to transform not just your marriage but your spouse's heart and yours, for your good and His glory.

God will help people who are willing to repent of broken trust and teach them how to be trustworthy. He understands feelings and will help with your emotions. He can heal broken trust, a broken heart, a broken spirit, broken lives, and broken marriages. He will never let you down. Trust Him, and learn to know Him more as you pray to Him and read His Word.

The hardest response and yet the most important is to pause and begin seeking the Lord. Know and remember right now what the Bible teaches us:

- **God loves you.**
  Let your face shine on your servant;
      save me in your unfailing love. (Psalm 31:16)

- **God will direct your paths.**
  Trust in the LORD with all your heart
      and lean not on your own understanding;
  in all your ways acknowledge him,
      and he will make your paths straight.
  (Proverbs 3:5–6)

- **God will give you the strength you need to do the right thing.**
  I can do everything through him who gives me
      strength. (Philippians 4:13)

- **God will provide for your needs.**
  And my God will meet all your needs according
      to his glorious riches in Christ Jesus.
  (Philippians 4:19)

- **God will give you wisdom.**
  If any of you lacks wisdom, you should ask God,
      who gives generously to all without finding
      fault, and it will be given to you. (James 1:5)

- **God is near to the brokenhearted.**
  The LORD is close to the brokenhearted
  and saves those who are crushed in spirit.
  (Psalm 34:18)

- **God assures us that in times of disaster, He is our safe place.**
  Have mercy on me, my God, have mercy on me,
  for in you I take refuge.
  I will take refuge in the shadow of your wings
  until the disaster has passed. (Psalm 57:1)

God is our refuge and strength. The Bible has many promises to hold on to by faith in difficult times. Strength will come from spending time daily reading from the Bible. As we spend time in prayer and seeking the Lord's will, He will guide. The Holy Spirit will provide comfort. God is our hope and our solid rock.

2

First Steps

God is our refuge and strength, an ever-present help in trouble.
—Psalm 46:1

An accident, injury, or tragic event happens. You have to go to the emergency room of a hospital. Once you're there, the doctors and nurses do triage to assess the situation and begin treatment. The medical staff act quickly and wisely to deal with the most urgent symptoms and then deal with other needs. They have to stop the bleeding and focus on life-threatening conditions first. Then they can address the other issues to improve your health and well-being.

In a similar way, when trust has been broken in a marriage and it comes to light, it is immediately an emergency situation. The couple and those stepping up to walk alongside to help should address the most urgent needs first. Then there can be systematic care given for other conditions that have to be considered and processed.

As emotions are surging and thoughts are whirling after broken trust has surfaced, it is hard to know what to do. What are the necessary first steps? It is essential for the couple and helpers to act with caution, discernment, and compassion. Maintain the big picture of what honors God, then begin on the specific steps that need to be sorted out. This requires patience and guidance to slow down impulsive reactions and provide the support for helpful measures.

Slow Down

A person's initial reaction is usually not the best response. What may seem at first to be the right reaction may prove not to be the best plan after the benefit of time, reflection, and godly counsel. Extreme emotions can lead to detrimental reactions. Commit to talking to an objective person before acting on impetuous ideas. Prevention is better than regrets. One wrong action does not justify another in response.

Struggling spouses may plan at the outset to just abandon the marriage and "bail out." This may have been a difficult marital situation for a long time. The spouse may not feel the emotional strength to continue. Those who are seeking to help this couple will want to encourage them to prayerfully and carefully take one step at a time.

First Peter 5:7 counsels, "Cast all your anxiety on him because he cares for you." Encourage them to pour their hearts out to God. He will listen and give comfort to them. Prayer is a very important means of knowing God's will. Pray regularly with a listening heart. Prayer switches the focus off the crisis and turmoil onto God and His faithfulness. Communicating with God brings comfort to a broken heart. Then wait to take any actions. As Psalm 27:14 exhorts, "Wait for the LORD; be strong and take heart and wait for the LORD."

Seek Help

Typically, when a couple find themselves in a crisis or trauma, they turn to others for help. Most commonly, the people they contact are close family members or dear friends. These are the people who may have known them as individuals before marriage and then as a couple. They are usually familiar with their relationship and care about them very much.

These significant friends and family members will encourage the couple to seek help from a godly, objective person who can help them navigate through these rough waters. This person can minister to them appropriately, address all the necessary aspects, see the relationship realistically, and cast a vision for a restored marriage.

Responding adequately and in a biblical way to what both the husband and wife are experiencing requires care and objectivity. It is difficult for friends and family members to address all the issues that need to be confronted, corrected, comforted, taught, guided, and changed.

Hopefully, these significant friends and family members can serve as precious encouragers and prayer partners for the couple. They are vital in these roles. They will not need to know all the facts or the details of the journey of restoration in order to fulfill their roles. Loved ones can share hope and faith in God that will greatly benefit the couple.

A friend or family member who can help calm any tendencies to act quickly will be a valuable support. Each spouse can check with such a person when inclined to take impulsive turns as events unfold. Be aware that information and emotions can rapidly trigger pain, resulting in possible hasty solutions and impetuous plans.

Many factors should be considered in responding to these heart-wrenching situations. Finding a person who understands how to minister to the couple, can offer biblical truth, and has a level of objectivity is the best combination. Biblical guidance is uniquely beneficial because it provides spiritual comfort and practical instruction for the couple. This person can be a minister, a biblical counselor, or a wise friend.

The situation the couple faces needs to be addressed in terms of context and perspective. *Context* means looking at the whole relationship. This involves looking at the marriage, precipitating factors and their frequencies, behavioral patterns, heart issues, relationship history, and other facts. Thorough exploration and discussion will bring clarification.

Bringing *perspective* means having the wisdom to look at the situation and the needs of the couple in view of what the Bible teaches. Those working with the couple can model and encourage how to respond kindly and biblically. There is too much at stake and the risks are too high for couples to be led in wrong directions.

Couples should use discernment before disclosing information to multiple people. A good rule of thumb is to share only with people who can bring positive help for the marriage. A tendency is to want to tell a number of people for prayer support and sympathy, or even out of anger. This is not wise because others continue to remember the problems and conflicts long after they have been resolved.

Sometimes there are circumstances in which the trust has been broken and unfaithfulness has occurred with both spouses. This means that both situations need to be processed wisely and thoroughly led through the steps toward restoration. Usually, this means dealing first with either the most current or the most extensive. However, it can be handled by a simultaneous and concurrent process of flexing back and forth to address all the issues.

It is human nature to think that another's sins are worse, more egregious and impactful, than one's own. Initially, each spouse feels more harmed by the sins of the other, and their own sins seem more minimal. It is important to help each one understand how God views all the sins that have been committed and how the sinful actions feel to each spouse.

Along the way the couple may be tempted to stop before the process has been completed. One of the most loving things friends and family members can do to help couples is to encourage them to continue through the process. Take necessary steps carefully and adequately. Couples who receive meaningful help have a greater chance for the most positive outcomes.

Trust God with the future even when you don't know what

is ahead. God will guide you. In the most difficult times of life, it is important to realize that we need God and turn to Him. This is especially true when one's marriage is hurting. God loves each spouse and marriage very much. As individuals seek Him, He gives strength, comfort and wisdom.

Let God's Word Give Hope and Guidance

God has a plan for the marriage, and that has not changed. Biblical guidelines are still more important than the sin, difficulties, and wrong actions that have happened. Hurting couples often say, "We've tried everything." However, that is not true if they haven't committed to focused, compassionate, biblical counseling. That is what can give hope and possibility for change.

> For the word of God is living and active. Sharper than any double-edged sword, it penetrates even to dividing soul and spirit, joints and marrow; it judges the thoughts and attitudes of the heart. Nothing in all creation is hidden from God's sight. Everything is uncovered and laid bare before the eyes of him to whom we must give account. (Hebrews 4:12–13)

God's Word is alive and active. It is relevant for your life today, and God speaks His truth through the Bible. There is tremendous power in the Word of God. God said through Isaiah that His Word "will not return to me empty, but will accomplish what I desire and achieve the purpose for which I sent it" (Isaiah 55:11).

The truth of the Bible is like a double-edged sword that cuts past our denials, deception, and sinfulness. It reveals the motives of the heart and judges what is right or wrong in the most hidden parts of our being. The Bible says that God knows everything, and we must give an accounting to Him.

"All Scripture is God-breathed and is useful for teaching, rebuking, correcting and training in righteousness" (2 Timothy 3:16). Paul taught that the Bible is inspired by God and is just what we need. He gave four ways that the Bible is useful, and each one is helpful when trust has been broken in marriage. *Teaching* shares instructing principles from God's Word that are absolute and sufficient for every situation in life. *Rebuking* confronts wrong actions in light of God's truth. *Correcting* reveals what are right and good thoughts, motives, and actions. *Training in righteousness* teaches how to do what is right. It trains one to have a life and marriage that pleases God.

The couple that is hurting desperately needs hope. The most powerful source of hope that they can ever experience is a personal relationship with Jesus Christ. Then the next greatest source of hope is the Bible. Reading through Psalms and many parts of God's Word reveals the greatness of God and His love and strength. The Bible provides wonderful comfort, strength, and guidance for the struggles of life. Let God and His Word bless your life.

> For everything that was written in the past was written to teach us, so that through endurance and the encouragement of the Scriptures we might have hope .... May the God of hope fill you with all joy and peace as you trust in him, so that you may overflow with hope by the power of the Holy Spirit. (Romans 15:4, 13)

The Word of God, the Bible, gives hope when we are hopeless. True wisdom and grace come from the Bible and God's Holy Spirit. The Bible has the answers for these very difficult challenges in life. Its truths are timeless and life changing. It is important to believe the Lord and seek wisdom and guidance from the Bible.

The Bible is practical and relevant to every part of life. Though it may not specifically speak to every precise circumstance in life, there are principles that can be applied to every part of life. God cares about our heart, our relationships (especially marriage), and every decision and action. When we seek Him and how to honor Him with our life, He guides us. Couples experience great joy as they see the truths from God's Word positively impacting their marriage.

The Holy Spirit leads us, and God's Word teaches about what is right and wrong and what to do. We can know His will by seeking wise counsel from Christians who love the Lord and want to obey Him. We can also receive guidance from godly people who love us and want what is best and right for us.

> So do not fear, for I am with you;
> > do not be dismayed, for I am your God.
> I will strengthen you and help you;
> > I will uphold you with my righteous right
> > hand. (Isaiah 41:10)

We can trust the Word of God, the Bible, to give clear and sound answers to hurting marriages and individuals. We can trust God to compassionately comfort, instruct, and empower those who are hurting deeply. When trust has been broken in marriage, your first steps are critical. Remember to slow down, seek help, and apply biblical truth. God is faithful and indescribably wonderful in how He comforts, instructs, and heals shattered hearts and lives.

3

Caught and Confronted

Nathan said to David, "You are the man!"
—2 Samuel 12:7

King David committed adultery with Bathsheba. Later, he had Uriah, her husband, killed on the front lines of battle. The Bible says, "The thing David had done displeased the LORD" (2 Samuel 11:27). David knew what he did was wrong. He went to great lengths to hide his sin and must have thought that he had gotten away with it. He felt guilt for his sin, but his pride led him to believe he could cover it up. He had no plans to confess.

In 2 Samuel 12:1, the Bible says that "the LORD sent Nathan to David" to confront him. Nathan boldly declared to King David, "Why did you despise the word of the LORD by doing what is evil in his eyes? You struck down Uriah the Hittite with the sword and took his wife to be your own" (2 Samuel 12:9). David was caught!

God loves us but hates our sin. He does not condone or allow it to be covered over and hidden. God knows that sin destroys, causing devastation to lives and relationships.

When a Spouse Is Caught Breaking Marital Trust

Many times when the trust is broken in marriage, the spouse is caught in some way. The whole tone of the situation when a spouse is caught is very different than if the person willingly confesses sin. When one is caught, immediate and long-term considerations come into play. These include the urgency of the situation, the components of what is happening, and the immediate steps that need to be taken.

Let's begin by defining that caught does not mean literally caught in the act. Rather, a broader definition means that something or someone other than the guilty spouse has brought the moral failure to light. Something happens that raises suspicion, and a closer look reveals the sin. Sometimes information emerges that a spouse is currently involved in a relationship, activity, or behavior that is contrary to the marriage vows.

Learning about the broken trust may follow a background of mistrust, doubt and questions. Typically, when a spouse is caught breaking marital trust, it can be presumed the spouse had no intention of confessing or ending the behavior. A spouse caught may say that he or she was planning to stop and report the misbehaviors. This seems questionable if no prior steps were taken in that direction. The declaration of intent may be an attempt to deflect the inconvenient revelations.

After it is found out that a spouse has done something that breaks the trust of the marriage, everything instantly focuses on that. Very strategic steps need to be taken to begin to sort things out. The sins have been done from a reckless and uncaring perspective toward the other spouse. The actions have been based on selfish desires or lustful cravings. The reactions when confronted may be the same.

When a spouse is breaking the trust of the marriage, he or she desires to keep the treacherous offenses hidden and protected. This requires strong levels of deception. The actions have been self-serving and focused on personal plans and decisions. The surprise of being caught or confronted can bring immediate retaliation and rage. "How dare you mess up my plans!" is the unspoken, idolatrous feeling.

Indicators and Information

Being caught often begins with evidence in e-mails, text messages, phone calls, pulling away, unaccountable time schedules, and secrecy. Whenever sin is unexpectedly confronted, the initial response is most often denial and lashing out at whoever is bringing the wrong to light. That person becomes the target of rage. The reaction usually morphs into anger, blaming the spouse, stirring up arguments, conflicts, denials, arrogance, excuses, and lies.

Perhaps you were looking through the credit card statements for the past few months and found purchases or cash advances that you did not know about. Possibly you were checking through the cell phone bills and noticed unfamiliar numbers appearing. E-mails may have appeared that are questionable or alarming.

Maybe you were chatting with a friend who casually commented that she thought she saw your husband with another woman at a quaint restaurant in a nearby suburb. Or on a normal day you received a phone call that shook your world. The person on the other end was revealing to you that they knew that your spouse was having an affair.

Perhaps your spouse has a heightened interest in fitness, weight loss, or beauty- and image-enhancing products and activities. These may be coupled with a feeling of distance in the marriage relationship. Maybe your spouse has criticized your own appearance. If a spouse has had frequent lengthy individual errands, less connection as a couple, and increased reluctance to respond to requests for communication or activities together, these may be warning signs.

Increased irritability, negative talk, excessive frustration, and less desire to solve problems or reconcile can be areas of concern. Selfish expectations, a contentious atmosphere, general unhappiness, a critical spirit, the lack of a serving, loving attitude, and reduced spiritual fruit all raise questions. Preoccupation, emotional detachment, and changes in schedules or eating and sleeping are all-noteworthy.

However the information comes to you, your world is turned upside down in a moment. The shock, rage, sorrow, fear, and confusion all simultaneously dump into a sickening mixture. At that moment it is completely overwhelming. Just as in other situations of receiving negative and possibly life-changing information, you are reeling and caught off balance emotionally.

The information may bring thoughts such as *Now it all makes sense, I should have known,* or *That's just like her.* Other thoughts and concerns are *What does this information mean, and what am I going to do with it?* The decisions that follow these questions will greatly impact the relationship and your life.

Confronting the Wrong

When Adam and Eve sinned in the garden of Eden by disobeying God's instructions, God confronted them. Adam and Eve tried to hide from God and hide their shame by covering themselves with fig leaves. However, the spiritual shame is removed only when a person confesses the sin to God and to the person sinned against and asks for forgiveness.

When a married partner finds out the spouse has broken the trust, confrontation is appropriate and necessary. Ignoring sin or avoiding dealing with it delays necessary attention to the relationship. If postponed, things can deteriorate quickly. Confrontation is not easy, but it is an act of love for the marriage.

"Brothers, if someone is caught in a sin, you who are spiritual should restore him gently. But watch yourself, or you also may be tempted" (Galatians 6:1). Paul taught that when someone is caught in sin, we have a spiritual responsibility to confront them for the purpose of restoration. A husband or wife may be fearful that if they confront their spouse, the marriage relationship will be harmed. But the relationship is already hurting very deeply, not because of the confrontation but because of the unfaithfulness.

Others may decide to ignore the unfaithfulness, telling themselves that it will take care of itself if nothing is said. It is not good for either spouse (or the relationship) to continue as if the breaking of trust did not happen and everything is normal. To think that the situation will just go away or take care of itself is naïve and delusory. When a spouse is caught, plans for appropriate confrontation need to be made. These are often best made with the help of an objective person or wise and caring family member.

When a spouse decides to confront, he or she needs to realize that one of the possible outcomes is that the offending spouse may choose not to repent and express that they want out of the marriage. When this is the case, it is wise not to react immediately but instead to give time for the Holy Spirit to work in the heart of the estranged spouse. Many can give testimony that their unrepentant spouse later had a change of heart and came to a place of genuine repentance.

Paul taught in Galatians 6:1 that the confrontation should be done *gently*. This word does not mean a spirit of leniency as if the sin did not matter. Instead it means that the confrontation is done appropriately and prayerfully. That is why Paul added, "But watch yourself, or you also may be tempted."

The method and timing of confrontation are very important and need to be decided in the most careful way. Determine in advance what you are going to say and what questions you will ask. It is beneficial to discuss the plans with a trusted confidant. Prepare yourself spiritually for the confrontation with prayer and Bible reading.

When facts and information begin to surface that reveal the broken trust, often assumptions are made and emotions quickly get out of control. The tendency is to react immediately and impetuously. Instead, base your response on facts, not on fears, incomplete conclusions, or impulses. Allow time to pass before making decisions.

> Therefore, if you are offering your gift at the altar and there remember that your brother has something against you, leave your gift there in front of the altar. First go and be reconciled to your brother; then come and offer your gift. (Matthew 5:23–24)

Be committed to take the initiative and address the wrong in a timely way. I think of this verse as teaching us "Don't wait on the other person, and don't wait around." We are not to wait for the other person to take the initiative to resolve the conflict. Some say, "I'll let the other person take the first step toward me." However, it is best to take the initiative.

Worshipping God is a theme of the Bible from Genesis to Revelation. Matthew 5:23–24 does not teach us that reconciliation is more important than worship. Rather, the lesson is that reconciliation is important and should be addressed in a timely way.

Addressing issues in relationships is acting in love toward the other person and the relationship. It honors God. That is especially true regarding broken trust in marriage. However, it will not be what the offending spouse desires. Typically, that person feels fairly confident that the secrets are safely tucked away. Unsuspectingly, the individual continues in the wrong behaviors.

Before anyone plans to confront their spouse, they need to be very sure that they have carefully thought through many aspects of the process. Considerations of timing, method, location, safety, questions, support measures, and ramifications are all significant. It is important to remember that when someone is caught doing wrong; they will be surprised about being found out or being confronted.

The component of timing is focused on what is best for the offended spouse, who will probably be doing the confronting. I say probably because under certain circumstances, it may be better if a third party or an objective person helps with the confronting or a major portion of it. The timing should be based on what's best for the hurting spouse when it comes to emotional stamina, convenience, and available support.

The untrustworthy spouse can manipulatively attempt to become the victim. He or she may say, "I feel like you're beating me up." The excuses and justifications seem to evolve into feeling "picked on" and that "it's just too hard for me to have to admit this—why do we have to talk about it?" Shifting the blame off the offenses and onto the confrontation is a common distraction. How firmly the offending spouse maintains this position may indicate how likely a timely confession may be.

Confronting betrayal means colliding with a heart of selfishness and deception. Expect to be met with blasting anger and denials. Human nature is ugly and harsh compared to what should be pure and loving. There is little regard for what is precious in God's sight and forgetfulness about what began as sacred. Unfaithfulness and broken trust violate the unique "oneness" that God intended for marriage. That's why the betrayal is so painful.

Marriage should be the strongest and most beautiful earthly relationship, but it sometimes isn't. Disregarding the marital covenant is destructive and devastating. Confrontation of broken vows and broken trust in marriage is one of the saddest experiences imaginable for a spouse. This is especially true when the faithful spouse wants to have a marriage that is filled with love and honor.

Even in the midst of this dark time, it is important to remember that God loves you. He will give you everything you need as you seek Him. He is your hope and strength. His peace and comfort will fill your heart and life. Trust in Him, and He will guide you and give you wisdom for going forward.

> The LORD is close to the brokenhearted
> and saves those who are crushed in spirit.
> (Psalm 34:18)
> God is our refuge and strength,
> an ever-present help in trouble. (Psalm 46:1)

4

Heart Conviction That Leads to Confession

He who conceals his sins does not prosper, but whoever
confesses and renounces them finds mercy.
—Proverbs 28:13

There are several differences regarding confession after a spouse
has been caught versus voluntary confession when offenses have
been kept secret for a time. Sometimes earlier in marriage a spouse
may have been unfaithful. At that time, the spouse made a choice
to keep those actions hidden. Not surprisingly, the Holy Spirit
convicts that person's heart to confess. Now after thought and
prayer, the spouse has decided to finally confess the offenses, even
though significant time has passed.

There will be concern about what the responses and impacts
will be. There will be temptations to avoid unsolicited confession.
However, continued secrecy is not positive for the spouse who is
keeping the secret or for the spouse who does not know. What
are the benefits of confessing the sins? What are the arguments to
justify secrecy? We will look at both these questions.

Unfaithfulness is always destructive to marriage. In fact,
infidelity can lead to divorce regardless of whether it was discovered
or voluntarily confessed. However, God is able to bring hope to a
marriage relationship even when it seems like a hopeless situation.

When spouses seek to obey God, their marriage has a greater potential for experiencing the blessings that God wants for them.

George and Monica wept after Monica told him that she had not been faithful in the marriage, though he had always believed she was. Monica had an affair earlier in their marriage and at that time decided to keep it a secret. Since then, she had felt conviction from the Holy Spirit and decided to confess, even though she knew George could possibly leave her. She hoped he wouldn't but felt strongly that telling him was the only fully honest thing to do and that he had a right to know. Monica told him everything, apologized, and asked for forgiveness. She made a new commitment to be completely faithful and transparent going forward.

George was deeply heartbroken but thankful for her honesty. He knew that Monica had been faithful and committed for several years now since the affair. He chose to stay committed to her. As they sought help from their pastor their marriage has begun to heal and become stronger than it ever was. Monica is no longer living in fear that her unfaithfulness will become known. She knew that either way it was going to be terribly hurtful to George, but it would have been even worse if he found out from someone else.

Rationalizations to Avoid Confession

Protecting Spouse from Additional Pain

There are different views regarding whether it's best or not to confess earlier undisclosed unfaithfulness. It can disrupt the marriage and cause pain for the spouse. Thoughts like *Don't disturb the peace, Keep the past in the past, Avoid hurting your spouse in a new way,* and *Avoid the confusion and sadness it can bring* are justifications for continued deception. What is the right thing to do?

Perhaps spouses recently attended a marriage conference that discussed being honest and confessing sins to each other. Or maybe the Holy Spirit convicted a spouse of the importance of confessing a previous time of dishonesty to the spouse. Possibly a spouse has been praying for the courage to confess past sinful actions to the other marriage partner.

An apparently strong marriage can suddenly be shocked and caught off guard. What if one of the spouses has engaged in destructive actions earlier in the marriage? That spouse has managed to keep those actions secret, even imagining that they will never be found out. Then something changes that. What if somehow they are found out, or the spouse becomes compelled to disclose?

Sometimes not confessing may seem kind and loving. The rationalization is to protect one's spouse from the painful truth. Some may think the difficulties of the disclosure will be greater than the good to be gained. It's tempting to ignore the wrongs and just commit to do better in the future. This is especially true if the marriage is going well now and the secret seems secure. Is this rationalization true? What does the Bible say?

> For whatever is hidden is meant to be disclosed,
> and whatever is concealed is meant to be brought
> out into the open. (Mark 4:22)

What if the Secret Were to Become Known?

Secret sins may seem to be carefully tucked away. However, it is unreliable to assume that they will remain secret. God often brings things to light in very surprising ways. It is wrong to assume that God does not care about complete honesty or past hidden sins. This is especially true in marriage, where trust is foundational. In the Bible, when King David committed adultery, God revealed his sins. God is a loving and pursuing Lord.

I have witnessed many amazing circumstances in which things

were revealed in the most unexpected ways. The secret keeper most often is flabbergasted at how supposed coincidences work together to bring truth to light. For the person who sinned, it is much better to confess than for the offenses to become known in other ways. For the faithful spouse, it is better to hear it directly from his or her marriage partner than to hear it from another person or find out in another way.

The Bible speaks to a person's heart through the Holy Spirit and convicts of the need to confess to their precious partner in marriage. God is righteous and never instructs people to do wrong. Maybe there is a desire to end the secrecy and come clean about past wrongs. Perhaps a spouse develops a desire to be obedient and honor God. A heavy heart and a desire for authentic marriage motivate toward confession.

It is often difficult to do the right thing. The desire to do right should be more compelling than doing what is easy. God calls us to a life of holiness and obedience. If we want to honor God and be all that He wants us to be, then that means following His commands even when humanly we would rather not. God calls us to act correctly, regardless of the cost. Faith means that we obey what the Bible teaches, trusting God with the outcome.

Some may argue that it is actually self-serving to confess past sins. They think confession would be driven by the selfish desire to get rid of cumbersome guilty feelings regardless of the impact on the other person. However, this is not what the Bible teaches. The Bible teaches that confession is doing what God says is right and loving toward others. Confession is to bring healing, not destruction.

> Therefore confess your sins to each other and pray for each other so that you may be healed. The prayer of a righteous person is powerful and effective. (James 5:16)

Reasons Why It Is Important

Confessing Sins Honors God

After confessing, strong reactions may cause one to wonder whether the confession was a mistake. Emotional and difficult responses should be expected. Even when the initial confession is painful, it is much better than hidden sin. Spouses regularly say that they would rather know the truth than to have a secret in the marriage. Calm measured responses will go far in modeling the love that should be motivating the confession.

When a spouse is ready to confess previously concealed sins, it is crucial to be completely honest and disclose fully. This is important for two reasons. First, it is obedience to God. Second, it shows love toward others. A person cannot be selective and only tell part of the truth, no matter how tempting that is. Any secrecy harms the trust in marriage. There is a risk to confessing past sins, but there would be a greater risk if they are not completely revealed.

Don't hold anything back. The objective of "coming clean" is not accomplished unless everything is admitted. Often confession may occur in a pastor's office or counselor's office to help with the initial response and help prepare the unsuspecting partner. Biblical counseling can help with the emotional aftermath.

Confessing Shows Love to the Spouse

Often a person says, "I don't want to hurt my spouse more, so I won't tell everything." Secrecy is more hurtful. Honesty builds trust. The commitment to obey God with disclosure must be greater than the fear of the difficulty it may present. Avoiding pain now is not the highest goal. Telling only part of the truth is another method of dishonesty and causes even more pain. To avoid complete truth would be acting from a self-protecting position. Love is willing and committed to complete honesty.

> Instead, speaking the truth in love, we will in all things grow up into him who is the Head, that is, Christ. (Ephesians 4:15)

Continuing the secrecy and hiding sins focuses on shortsighted goals of protecting self more than loving the spouse or the Lord. Imagine if two people had an affair and then it ended. The secret was hidden away, and neither person told anyone. We can know that God will be convicting both to confess it. What if one is finally obedient to confess? Or what if God allows the truth to be revealed in some way as only He can?

Wouldn't it have been better if each partner had confessed to his or her own spouse? No one can assume that secrets won't be told or that they won't be revealed in unimaginable ways. God is righteous and intent about laying bare the truth. He does not wink at sin or brush it aside. Never underestimate His pursuing love. Know that it is always better to correct something after the fact than not at all.

When it becomes known, the offended spouse will rightfully ask, "Why did you not tell me this earlier?" "Why did you share a secret with someone outside our marriage without telling me?" "When you stopped the sin to recommit to our marriage, why didn't you tell me the truth then?" The actions of the unfaithfulness and the sin of not admitting sooner should both be included in the confession.

When spouses are asked if they want to be kept out of a secret involving the spouse and someone outside the marriage, they say "No!" A faithful spouse, when given a choice, will usually prefer to know all the facts instead of being lied to or having any deception continue. This is even true if the truth is hurtful. Marriage partners want to be informed regarding their spouse and marriage. If the roles were switched, the other spouse would want to know as well. Treat your spouse the same way that you would want to be treated.

> Do to others as you would have them do to you.
> (Luke 6:31)

Confessing after Conviction by the Holy Spirit Strengthens Marriage

The Bible teaches that confessing sins to one another is a first step toward healing. Sin injures relationships. God brings healing as sins are confessed with commitments for repentance. God blesses when people confess. Humility that leads to confession rebuilds trust and confidence in a spouse's heart.

Confession does not negate the positive things in the marriage. Initially, the other spouse may fear that everything else in the marriage has been dishonest or deceptive. However, although there are past sins and offenses, which have now been confessed, these do not negate the other positive aspects of the marriage. These special times include children, events, and memorable times.

A spouse may doubt whether anything is good that has occurred between the sin and the confession. "If this happened when I thought things were good, how can I trust anything now? Everything must be a lie." However, this is not a correct conclusion. Current confession does not take away the authentic good of what had previously occurred. When the spouse has been faithful and trustworthy in the marriage between the wrong actions and the confession, the marriage and the positive history is still something to affirm and a source of solace.

Special Considerations When Confessing Wrongs Based on Leading from the Holy Spirit

The Holy Spirit leads to confession. When this happens after a time lapse, the confession should be handled with care, tenderness, and humility. Careful steps must be implemented. The confession will be regarding actions from earlier in the relationship that remained undisclosed. However, when these actions are revealed to the faithful spouse for the first time, it immediately becomes new information. The flood of emotions feels very current. It is important that the confessing spouse and those who are helping the couple be compassionate regarding this.

The confessing spouse must lay aside defensiveness and communicate humbly. Care for the spouse who has just learned that the trust was broken. When confessing, accept full responsibility and acknowledge your own wrongs. As difficult as it may seem to the one confessing past wrong actions, it is much harder for the offended spouse who is hearing this new information.

Expect that the news will be shocking and disturbing. Focus on the past wrong actions that brought the needed confession, not the reactions to the confession. It would be counterproductive and insensitive to react inappropriately to the hurt felt by the faithful spouse. The purpose of the confession is to be honest and loving, so the way it is handled should match that.

If the confession is met with a strong reaction from the spouse, one can easily be tempted to say, "Look at how you are acting. See, that's why I didn't confess to you sooner." Or "Think about me. It's pretty hard to confess, and now you are blasting me. You should be glad I'm being honest now. Next time I just won't tell you." "I should have known you wouldn't understand."

All of these are very bad statements and sabotage everything good about the long overdue confession. They would all be extremely harmful and also dishonest. The truth is that the reason the confession did not happen sooner was only to protect self, not the spouse. To threaten future deception is manipulative. This is not the time for self-praise for the "courageous and noble" confession or for a victim mentality to creep in.

The confession will be meaningful only if it is truly humble and sorrowful about the sins. Do not let it morph into self-centered concern. Do not fall into the temptation to praise self or to instruct or correct the confused and hurting spouse. It is hypocritical to shift the focus to how the spouse is reacting. The focus should stay on the past wrong behaviors, with a willingness to confess fully, apologize, commit to repentance, and ask for forgiveness.

When a person is intentional to confess sins, it is the culmination of much thought and prayer. This person feels conviction from the Holy Spirit and wants to be obedient. Hopefully, the confessing spouse will have a driving desire to do what is right and to do it in the best way. Wise counsel can guide that appropriately.

The spouse who is hearing the confession for the first time will experience shock, hurt, anger, fear, confusion, doubt, and profound sadness. It is beneficial for the confessing spouse to have a person present who can help the faithful spouse when hearing the confession. The hurting spouse should understand that the confessing spouse is trying to be obedient to biblical principles. Sometimes there may be a feeling of vindication if there were suspicions in the past.

Benefits of Confessing after Heart Conviction

Proactive confessions remove the risk that past secrets could become known in ways that would jeopardize the trust in a marriage. To have the truth disclosed by a spouse is better than having it revealed from another source. Honesty is best and allows the marriage to reestablish a foundation of integrity and credibility. It strengthens the assurance and security of the marriage. The desire is toward healing. Though confession is the right action, no guarantee can be made regarding the response of the other spouse.

It is a wrong assumption for a spouse to avoid confession because of the misconception that the marriage will be healthier with the secret hidden. In the same way it is a wrong assumption for a person to avoid seeking medical help assuming that he or she will be healthier if an illness is undiagnosed and untreated.

Confession in marriage can allow for potentially effective health and growth. It can strengthen it to be the marriage that God intends.

Sheila and Lester were asked to share their testimony at church. Their marriage has recently gone through growth in surprising ways. Six months ago, Lester confessed to Sheila that he had been involved in an affair several years earlier with a former high school friend he had connected with on Facebook. He had stopped the affair but then chose to keep it hidden from Sheila. However, the Lord impressed him to confess it to Sheila. After much anguish and prayer, he told her everything.

At first it was uncertain what would happen to the marriage. Sheila was shocked and brokenhearted. She did not know what to do. She talked with her pastor and began to realize how much faith and courage Lester showed to confess to her and that God can heal a marriage after unfaithfulness. Just as God had convicted his heart to confess, God also led Sheila to forgive and to stay committed to Lester. Since then, their marriage has grown deeper and more loving and trusting in wonderful ways.

When sin occurs, there must be confession. Even if the confession has been delayed and the sins were in the past, confessing sins is still the right thing to do. God loves each person, and He blesses when someone confesses present or past sins. Confession includes seeking God's forgiveness and the forgiveness of those harmed. When the truth is fully known, healing and restoration can begin.

> When I kept silent,
>   my bones wasted away
>   through my groaning all day long.
> For day and night
>   your hand was heavy upon me;
>   my strength was sapped
>   as in the heat of summer.

Then I acknowledged my sin to you
    and did not cover up my iniquity.
I said, "I will confess
    my transgressions to the LORD."
And you forgave
    the guilt of my sin. (Psalm 32:3–5)

5

Disclosure

Do not lie to each other, since you have taken off your old
self with its practices and have put on the new self, which is
being renewed in knowledge in the image of its Creator.
—Colossians 3:9–10

Disclosure is the process of speaking the truth, cleaning out, and
bringing things to light. For years, I've used an illustration with
couples regarding the importance of full and honest disclosure. I
would say it is like having an infection or cancer on your arm that
needs to be cleaned out for complete healing. I would use a motion
with my right arm toward my left arm as if I were cleaning it out.

Then, a few years ago, I developed a small lump on my left
arm in the same place I had used the illustration. After I'd gone
to doctors and had surgery to clean it out adequately, the biopsy
revealed a premalignant tumor. Though the surgery and recovery
were not pleasant, the result was worth it. Each time I look at that
scar, I am reminded of the importance of cleaning out harmful
things. That is also vital in a marriage.

Importance of Disclosure

Disclosure is necessary for marriages when the trust has been broken. It is an essential beginning step in the restoration process. Honesty and a willingness to disclose are required for the possibility of future marital healing. The disclosure must be forthright, complete and proactive.

Disclosure is the revealing of evidence and facts regarding prior deception or secrecy in the marriage. It includes information about people, places, and actions related in any way to the unfaithfulness or untrustworthiness. Disclosure can even come from others outside the marriage.

Disclosure differs from confession. Confession is an acknowledgement of personal wrongdoing, intentions, attitudes, motives, and heart issues that led to breaking the trust in marriage. Confession involves humility and remorse. While disclosure does not go as far as confession, it is a necessary element of it.

The offending spouse may think, *What you don't know won't hurt you.* He may seek the easy way out by avoiding disclosure, even claiming it is out of care for the spouse. But limiting or procrastinating on disclosure is neither honest nor loving. It blocks full healing in the marriage.

All the facts need to be revealed early on. As more information comes to mind, it should be disclosed to the spouse in a complete and honest manner. Avoiding disclosure and also saying, "I want to come clean," are contradictory.

> The LORD detests lying lips,
>> but he delights in men who are truthful.
>> (Proverbs 12:22)

Commitment to Honesty

The majority of spouses who have been hurt want everything disclosed. Some may appear reluctant at first to hear the full truth, either to spare the offending spouse or oneself the pain of full disclosure. However, soon they say, "Everything has to be revealed. I want to know everything. If you are not completely honest now, how will I be able to trust you in the future?" Partial truths equal dishonesty.

The hurting spouse, not the unfaithful spouse, needs to be the one who decides how much should be disclosed. Unfolding information and all that has transpired is a meticulous job and takes diligence. When facts begin to surface, the tendency is to gloss over some and get through the process as rapidly as possible.

A person with a commitment to disclose may say, "It's not going to be pretty, but I will tell you everything." If that is an honest statement, it will encourage the offended spouse. When a difficult bit of information is about to be shared, the unfaithful spouse may give a warning, saying, "Please be prepared. What I am about to tell you is especially difficult or hurtful."

Disclosure Excuses

"I don't want to hurt my spouse anymore."

It is common to hear, "I don't think it's good to disclose everything. I don't want to hurt you anymore." On the surface this sounds like a sincere concern for the spouse. However, on closer examination, the real motivation is often selfishness. The desire not to hurt the spouse should have led to avoiding the unfaithfulness in the first place. The same selfishness that originally led to sin is now evading honesty and transparency.

As disclosure begins, the hurting spouse is understandably brokenhearted. Perceiving this, the offending spouse may respond with "This is so difficult for you. I don't want to cause more pain." She is hopeful this response will sound convincingly loving and thus negate the need for any further admission or revelation. But the offending spouse lacks sincerity because self-preservation is often the true motivation.

Yes, disclosure is difficult for the hurting spouse. It is never easy to hear descriptions of sin and wrong actions committed against you. But it is even more difficult to know something happened but not know exactly what happened. Thus, hurting spouses should prepare themselves emotionally for the disclosure because the offending spouse's sin will be laid bare and the offended spouse's emotional response will be raw.

Sadly, the faithful spouse is often the last one to know about the unfaithfulness. The secrecy sometimes involves someone from the couple's community. Perhaps others in their community even witnessed the spouse's wrongdoing. Hearing it from someone else, or hearing it after the fact, crushes the heart and causes embarrassment. An unfaithful spouse who is unwilling to disclose may also in fact be unrepentant.

Marshall and Jane were seeking to restore their marriage after his unfaithfulness. He protested, "What's the benefit of disclosing?" He was thinking only of himself. Later, when Jane was struggling emotionally over all the information he had revealed, Marshall responded, "See, I knew I should not have confessed."

In reality, it was the magnitude of his sins that caused her so much sorrow, not the confession of them. Keeping deceptive actions hidden does not strengthen a marriage. With Marshall's continued evasiveness about his sin, Jane realized that he was not willing to change. She tired of his dishonesty and made the decision to end the marriage.

Sometimes, if caught in unfaithfulness, one may say, "I'm glad to be found out." However, that person may easily slip into anger over being caught when relational repercussions ensue. Relief over the deception being exposed turns to anger with the new awareness of all that will be expected by the offended spouse. Most never intend to have their secret actions revealed, and so there is often anger that their sinful frivolities have been interrupted.

The heart of the offending spouse can vacillate between acknowledging the wrongs committed and blaming the whistleblower or others. He can grasp at excuses for sin that short-circuit the process of reconciliation and only share enough to prevent his wife from seeking a divorce.

"Full disclosure will make it harder to forgive."

Often people think that confession will make it harder for the offended spouse to forgive. However, the opposite is true. The more proactive and prompt an offending spouse is in disclosing completely to a hurting spouse, the easier it will be for forgiveness to be given and restoration to occur. When a hurting spouse has the confidence that there are no more secrets and the offending spouse is genuinely remorseful and repentant, forgiveness comes more easily.

Even other family members who care about the couple are quicker to forgive when there is full disclosure and repentance. Humility, honesty, disclosure, and the commitment to do all that is necessary to rebuild broken trust are evidences of genuine brokenness and appropriate contrition. The presence of these will be evident to everyone. When the offending spouse says, "I will do whatever it takes for as long as it takes to rebuild your trust," the hurting spouse feels hope.

Detours to Disclosure

Overreaction

Sylvia learned her husband, John, was having an affair. She said, "Tell me everything." As John confessed, her anger increased.

"I can't take this. It makes me want to die," she responded. Her reaction placed John in a quandary. He wanted to be honest but did not want her to harm herself. Threatening suicide, lashing out in retaliation, and unwisely involving the children became her game plan.

Yes, the emotional pain was immense, but a destructive response is not an appropriate option. Even in the midst of one of the greatest struggles a marriage can ever face, there is still a wise and right way to respond. A dangerous backlash will not lead to a desired outcome. Being tempted to retaliate is understandable, but it would be wrong to do so. A biblical counselor can guide and encourage the healthy management of emotions.

Protecting the Offending Spouse

Sometimes the faithful spouse is so glad the offending spouse is back that full disclosure is overlooked. He may want the full truth but doesn't want the revelations to be too hard on the unfaithful spouse. In the effort to alleviate pressure, priorities can get confused and the hurting spouse can circumvent disclosure. When he becomes protective of the unfaithful spouse, the offender becomes the victim. "Going easy" on the unfaithful spouse is not good for either person.

Someone who has been hiding wrong actions will welcome anything that delays disclosure—especially when it surprisingly comes from the spouse they have greatly sinned against. This can happen in a number of different scenarios. But an objective third party can encourage the hurt spouse to pursue full disclosure. Disclosure is biblical and best for both the faithful and the unfaithful spouse.

Connie caught Sylvester in a homosexual affair. She was devastated but wanted a quick fix. She sabotaged full disclosure by saying she just wanted to save the marriage. She said she had forgiven him and wanted to focus on reconciliation. Sylvester was not sorry and did not disclose, confess, or repent. He knew she wanted to hang on to him and the marriage, no matter what. So he manipulated and blamed Connie for everything, and his sinful life continued.

> He who conceals his sins does not prosper,
>> but whoever confesses and renounces them
>> finds mercy. (Proverbs 28:13)

Extreme Preliminary Statements

One extreme statement that a spouse may make is "I can forgive a lot, but if you ever actually have sex with someone else, I'm divorcing you." That may be said at the beginning of a marriage as a deterrent to unfaithfulness, but be careful not to draw a line with no return. Sometimes there is sexual unfaithfulness in marriage. However, that does not mean that divorce is necessary. When there is repentance, restoration is often possible.

A second common statement is "I am committed to my marriage no matter what. I will never divorce my spouse." When this statement is made too hastily, it may in effect give a pass to the spouse who has broken trust. Feeling off the hook, one may hunker down, refuse to disclose, and dodge restoration until it all blows over. The best advice is not to say either of these extreme statements.

Disclosing in Limited Amounts

Inconsistent information during disclosure causes red flags and concerns. Changing facts, distractions, and sidestepping all circumvent progress and dishearten the hurting spouse even more. It is always best to tell everything early on. It hurts less to get it all out at once. The trickle method causes greater harm. The full truth is easier to deal with than imagined fears or bits and pieces at a time.

After broken trust has become exposed, there may be a stated willingness to admit to everything. But, over the next few days and weeks, disclosure may halt. The one who said earlier she would fully disclose changes her mind and is now hopeful that she won't have to do so. She stalls by trying to avoid any meaningful conversation about the sin she has committed. After beginning to disclose, then she may say, "That's all!" The hurting spouse feels relief and welcomes the pause.

Thus, those working with the couple should not assume that everything has been revealed. The initial disclosure almost always involves underreporting. Human nature is fiercely self-protective and deceptive. Encourage the offended spouse to brace for more as the earlier temporary relief can rapidly change to shock and deep pain again. "This is so hard. Just tell me everything now," is a frequent desperate plea.

Often an offending spouse will disclose in a very detailed way about some elements of the unfaithfulness. Then he will deliberately continue to hide other facts and be unwilling to disclose fully, hoping the spouse will believe he has been completely honest. Then he will often say, "Of course I am being completely honest. If I wanted to hide anything, why would I have given you all those other details." However, he is still continuing his selfish, sinful deception.

Expect Ups and Downs during Disclosure

Drama

One sign that someone is avoiding disclosure is drama. Frank caught Amanda in an affair with a neighbor. Amanda said she wanted to recommit to the marriage but avoided disclosure in every way possible. She was melodramatic and self-consumed: "I can't do this. This is just too hard. I don't understand why this is necessary. Frank doesn't want to hear this. Can't he just forgive me and move on? Dredging all this up isn't helpful for anyone."

Her solution was to affirm, "Everything's all right now. I'm not going to do it anymore. Our marriage is okay, and there's nothing to talk about." Those statements were untrue and out of touch with reality. Nothing had been talked through. Frank was emotionally weary of her lack of commitment. He was suspicious of her continuing flirtatious behaviors. Ultimately, Frank gave up on the marriage because he had no emotional energy to continue.

Shifting Blame and Distorting Facts

When a marriage partner lies or fudges on the truth, the spouse and others should confront it. The offending spouse will shift the focus to his spouse's actions or issues to make her the culprit and himself the victim. Statements like "You're not perfect either" distract from the issue of broken trust and shift the blame to the unoffending spouse.

A wife wanting to continue a deceptive affair makes excuses for all her wrong behaviors: "I want out of the marriage," "We have too many issues to resolve," "It's too little too late," "I don't love you anymore," "Nothing will ever change," or "I never really loved you." These common excuses throw salt on the wound and reveal a stubborn, defiant heart and lack of commitment.

> A truthful witness does not deceive,
>> but a false witness pours out lies. (Proverbs 14:5)

Laziness and Selfishness

Self-preservation by the offending spouse must be replaced with genuine sorrow for his sins. *I choose to be honest* should overpower the thought *I choose the easiest thing for me.* A manipulative spouse tries to convince the hurting spouse that "Less disclosure is better for you." But this hypocritical lie is intended to cover up laziness, sinfulness and self-protection.

The one who broke the trust in the marriage is hardly the expert in what is best for the marriage. A common reply from the offended spouse is "If you really cared about my best interests, why did you sin so tragically in the first place? That's when you should have thought about not wanting to hurt me."

Taking the path of least resistance does not lead to a healthy marriage. Healing and renewed commitment require biblical steps of growth. When spouses desire to honor God above all else, it is amazing the great things that happen in a marriage. Honoring the Lord and wanting a godly marriage are worth the effort and perseverance to seek what is holy.

Disclosure Procedures

Set a Time to Disclose

When the issue of broken trust surfaces, questions come fast and furiously. They are often expressed randomly 24/7. This all-consuming approach makes it difficult for the couple to function in their relationship and other responsibilities. There needs to be a plan to sort through the information while continuing in their daily life. Setting up designated information gathering times is helpful.

As a couple, set times for disclosure and discussion. Choose a time that will be good for each of you physically and emotionally, with no distractions or interruptions. Begin with sixty to ninety minutes, possibly twice or three times a week. At the end of each session, the couple can agree on the next disclosure time. The process will be emotionally exhausting, so take breaks as needed. You may have to end the conversation earlier than planned and resume it again at the next earliest opportunity. This allows time to think, pray, clarify the questions, and cope with the emotions.

Prepare a Chronological Narrative

Often an offending spouse will say, "You can ask me anything you want to. I will answer all your questions." While that sounds like an open and cooperative statement, it is actually lazy and evasive. The faithful spouse cannot possibly think of all the right questions to ask in order to get the necessary information. It is not his or her responsibility to do that, and it is too emotionally taxing.

The offended spouse should not have to fish for information. An unfaithful spouse is aware of the questions that need to be answered and knows what needs to be revealed. So he must be proactive about sharing information in a full and forthcoming way. Rebuilding trust requires absolute preparedness and motivation to tell the whole truth. But hesitancy or incomplete revelation is a deterrent to trust being restored.

Before disclosure times begin, the offending spouse should write a complete and thorough chronological narrative of everything pertaining to the broken trust. Start at the beginning and include all the details. The offending spouse must take the initiative and do the heavy lifting for full disclosure to occur. The information that is shared should be all-inclusive, forthright, and free flowing.

Begin the disclosure time with prayer. The offending spouse can then give a copy of the written chronological narrative to the offended spouse and read it out loud. The faithful spouse can ask questions along the way, go through the prepared statement one part at a time, or jot down reminders of what to ask later while listening to the whole statement first. Listening to the full narrative first may limit or clarify the questions that will be asked later.

Be aware that the information will cause pain. However, withholding needed information is even more destructive. The spouse who needs to disclose should not in any way be impatient or defensive. It may not be possible to go through the whole statement and all the questions in one meeting, so schedule disclosure times as frequently as needed.

The faithful spouse has the prerogative to ask anything she wants about the actions and events that have led to the broken trust. Pray about the questions to ask and what information you need and want to know. Ask open-ended questions as much as possible. Ask for details as needed.

Whenever the faithful spouse asks a question, the offending spouse knows what the spouse wants to know and should answer the questions completely. Do not give partial or limited information. Do not sidestep or avoid the truth.

Some Questions to Ask

Some important questions to ask would be about gifts the unfaithful spouse gave to the person she was unfaithful with, any promises she made, and the content of what she talked about with the person. If gifts were given, what they were and when they were given are significant facts. In adulterous relationships, gifts are commonly given, even gifts that had never been given in the marriage. This adds to the depth of betrayal but absolutely needs to be revealed. In the restoration process, giving meaningful gifts to the injured spouse can be a significant help.

What statements of affection and commitment were made? What promises or secret agreements were made? Were there conversations about divorcing the spouse and marrying the adulterous partner in the future? What plans about the future were discussed? In the midst of affairs, the offending spouse sometimes says negative things about the spouse, whether true or not. These are very hurtful. Whatever was said about the spouse that was negative needs to be confessed and apologized for. Facts are often easier to deal with than what one imagines happened.

Polygraph Test

When the offending spouse is for whatever reason reluctant to disclose completely, or if the faithful spouse doubts that everything has come out, he or she can ask for a polygraph test to be given to the unfaithful spouse. This can also be requested when the faithful spouse does not believe what has been disclosed. Polygraph tests can facilitate accountability and the rebuilding of trust.

The faithful spouse and a counselor can determine together the questions to be asked without the offending spouse knowing what they are in advance. Hopefully, the hurting spouse is able to meet with the person who will be administrating the lie detector test to go over the questions before the test is given. It is important that the offending spouse discloses everything before the lie detector test is implemented. No one wants a spouse to fail a polygraph test.

Benefits and Blessings

Disclosure is difficult because it goes against human nature and our proclivity to hide sin. However, the act of disclosure expresses obedience to God and is absolutely crucial before any progress can be made toward restoration in marriage. When disclosure is complete and honest, it allows a couple to begin moving toward reconciliation. It produces emotional energy to move forward in the next steps of growth and healing.

> Therefore each of you must put off falsehood and speak truthfully to his neighbor, for we are all members of one body. (Ephesians 4:25)

Part 2

Rebuilding

6

Confession

If I had cherished sin in my heart, the
Lord would not have listened.

—Psalm 66:18

In the Bible, after Nathan confronted David with his sin, there were many ways that he could have responded. David could have denied it all and continued to lie. He could have rationalized his sin and found others to blame. The Bible records that King David responded with the simple confession, "I have sinned against the Lord" (2 Samuel 12:13). David was called a man after God's own heart (1 Samuel 13:14). When confronted with his sin, he chose to acknowledge it, confess, and repent.

Confession means agreeing with God about sin, seeing it as He sees it. God sees sin as against Him and others. God sees sin as what caused His Son, Jesus Christ, to come to earth and have to die a horrific death on our behalf. Sin is harmful to others and self. Confession is the truthful acknowledgement and admission of wrong attitudes and actions that are contrary to the Bible, dishonoring and disobedient to God, and hurtful toward others.

Confession requires having an attitude of humility, dropping a guard of defensiveness, ceasing to conceal the sins, and bringing the offenses to light. Confession means realizing the magnitude of sin and how destructive it can be. Confession does not try to explain or put sin in the best light. Genuine confession involves a change of heart. Instead of focusing on hiding sin, justifying ourselves, and minimizing the destruction; we see the immense pain and devastation sin has produced.

Avoiding Confession

Some of the identifiable patterns of avoiding meaningful confession of sin are predictable and obvious. The temptation not to face our sins comes in several ways. The patterns of denying, rationalizing, minimizing, and justifying are clear indicators that there is push back against genuine disclosure and complete confession. None of these options lead to obedience to God or showing love to others. Instead, the focus is on protecting self.

Denial is the rejection of personal responsibility and refusal to acknowledge wrong actions. It is a basic form of avoidance and hinders any meaningful progress after sin has been found out. It is as elementary as a child who continues lying saying they are innocent when it is obvious they are not. It is pathetic to see an adult act that way, and it is devastating to a spouse who wants to take steps toward restoration. It is immature and detrimental.

Rationalization is the process of making excuses for actions that are selfish and wrong and break the trust in marriage. Often spouses will spend a great deal of time and effort explaining reasons for their terrible actions, hoping that they will be considered less offensive. Some people have the mind-set that if they continue to explain their perspective, then surely they will be vindicated at some point, and their actions will be understood.

Minimizing is the act of trying to convince others that our actions are really not so bad. It takes the position that people are overreacting to our sins, which should be considered minor. Comparing our actions to others may hopefully make ours more acceptable and even understandable. The hypocritical statement often is "It could be a lot worse. At least I'm not like the person that is doing even more."

Justifying is trying to color our wrongful actions as potentially or partially good. "It was when I was helping you by taking the kids to school that I met that other woman." "It was because I had gotten a job that you requested that caused me to become sexual with my boss." Justifying is the attempt to deny personal responsibility by placing the blame for the circumstances of the sinful action on the spouse or on one's own desire to do something good. "I was working late to make more money for us when I got sidetracked and responded to his advances."

All these techniques are very far from how God wants us to respond when we've sinned against Him and others. The first step the Lord expects is to admit the wrong actions and attitudes without any stalling or avoiding. God expects us to take the initiative and be forthright to disclose completely and honestly. A person must see the treachery of their actions. There must be humility with recognition of the pain inflicted. The way to act in love now is to have greater concern for those who have been hurt.

Biblical Confession

> Then I acknowledged my sin to you
> and did not cover up my iniquity.
> I said, "I will confess
> my transgressions to the LORD."
> And you forgave
> the guilt of my sin. (Psalm 32:5)

David described his confession in Psalm 32 and gives a model of biblical confession. Before his confession, he was groaning under the conviction of his sin. Day and night he felt the heavy weight of his guilt leaving him with no strength (verses 3–4). This all changed for David when he genuinely confessed his sin. His confession was not partial but complete.

David used three different phrases to describe his confession: "acknowledged … did not cover up … I will confess." He also used three words to describe his sin: "my sin … my iniquity … my transgressions." He took full responsibility for his sin. After his confession and asking God for forgiveness, he declared God's faithfulness.

God is holy. As Christians, we are called to live holy lives. God will not allow us to continue in sin without confronting us. His Holy Spirit convicts us and calls us to confession and repentance. Being convicted of sin by the Holy Spirit is a great blessing. At the time, conviction feels painful, not positive. However, it is proof of a loving and pursuing God working in your life.

What a blessing to realize that God cares so much about you that He personally speaks to you through His Spirit, inviting you to pray to Him, confess sins, and receive His forgiveness. We should not run from God but respond willingly when He draws us to Himself. A spouse should be willing to be fully honest and obey God even if the marriage is not restored.

> Therefore confess your sins to each other and pray for each other so that you may be healed. The prayer of a righteous man is powerful and effective. (James 5:16)

This verse teaches that confessing sins to each other is a major element for healing in relationships. It also says that confession impacts the effectiveness of our prayers. The Bible instructs us to confess our sins to each other so we can be healed. In order for a marriage to be healed from past offenses, confession and repentance have to take place. Even if one spouse has been "in the dark" regarding them, true healing can only come if the spouse acknowledges, confesses, and asks for forgiveness.

> Why do you look at the speck of sawdust in your
> brother's eye and pay no attention to the plank in
> your own eye? How can you say to your brother,
> "Let me take the speck out of your eye," when all
> the time there is a plank in your own eye? You
> hypocrite, first take the plank out of your own eye,
> and then you will see clearly to remove the speck
> from your brother's eye. (Matthew 7:3–5)

It is easy to focus on the speck in someone else's eye while
overlooking the plank in one's own eye. This is especially true
when one's actions come under scrutiny. Genuine confession does
not include blaming the other person. Another's actions or lack
of them do not cause one's sin. Everyone sins because he or she
chooses to sin. There are other issues in a hurting marriage that
will need to be addressed at the proper time. However, confession is
bringing one's own sin into the open and taking full responsibility
for it.

Meredith suspected that Ronnie was having an affair because
of many late-night meetings at his office. She found a repeated
unfamiliar number on his phone. Meredith looked at his office
directory and narrowed the strange number to a certain employee.
When Ronnie was confronted with the information, he lashed
out at her, "I'll never be able to trust you again." Ronnie accused
Meredith of being the one who had done wrong for finding the
phone number. He completely ignored his adulterous behavior and
made her investigation the offense. Meredith had every prerogative
to check out the phone numbers on his phone.

Responding to the Holy Spirit

After sinning, feelings of guilt can be very strong, and how a
person responds is crucial. Conviction that comes from the Holy
Spirit is based upon the truth about God's righteousness and sin.

The conviction of the Holy Spirit is a gift of love from the Lord and a beautiful invitation to confess sins to experience His grace and forgiveness. It is important to be responsive to the Holy Spirit. This requires a humble heart.

The temptation is to remain self-protective and hold on stubbornly to lies, excuses, and pride. To ignore or dismiss the gentle drawing of the Holy Spirit can lead someone down the path away from righteousness. Apart from God and His grace, we have no means of dealing with sin. We are hopeless and powerless to correct any wrong. However, when we confess and repent of our sin, God forgives us and restores us (1 John 1:9).

How a person responds to the apparent evidences that actions have broken the trust of the marriage reveals the person's heart. The actions that follow will clearly show if that person is remorseful about the sin and willing to disclose and confess completely and take steps with humility. Or the actions will indicate avoidance and further deception. Is the spouse confessing willingly or looking for ways to ignore or distract?

Heart issues need to be addressed and acknowledged in confession. What are the motivations of the heart? How has selfishness driven the desires and eclipsed a commitment to love God and act in love to others? How have worldly pleasures and lusts had preeminence over spiritual commitments and convictions?

A common statement by an unfaithful spouse is "I wasn't looking for an affair." This deflecting statement is most often untrue. Affairs result from inappropriate interactions without necessary safeguards in place. One may not have been intentional about seeking an affair. However, neither were there protections or obstacles to protect against incoming temptations. Sincere confession is honest, addresses these false statements, and acknowledges heart motivations.

Sexual sin is a form of idolatry. Sexual idolatry is worship of self by being consumed with personal desires for sexual pleasure and gratification. God wants each person to be sexually pure. The

Lord's guidelines are established for protection and maintenance of the sanctity of God's design for sexual activity and intimacy. Each person is created to honor God with everything in life, including sexual aspects. The worldly belief that sexual sin is harmless and insignificant is one of the biggest lies ever told. For a marriage, it has some of the most destructive results as it tears the deepest fibers of the marriage relationship.

> Put to death, therefore, whatever belongs to your earthly nature: sexual immorality, impurity, lust, evil desires and greed, which is idolatry. (Colossians 3:5)

Confession is uncomfortable but fundamentally important. Confession is more than just recounting facts of events and actions. It should also include heart issues. Confession acknowledges one's seeking after wrong actions and one's thoughts consumed with selfish lusts. Apart from full and honest confession, there cannot be genuine repentance. Without sincere repentance, there cannot be restoration. Confession is the primary step toward the potential healing of the marriage and the rebuilding of trust.

Sometimes people are more sorrowful about personal consequences than about the devastating repercussions of sins on others. Real sorrow about sin is not based on personal embarrassment or consequences. Rather, it is most significantly felt when realizing the impacts of the sinful actions on the people who are affected. Additional genuine remorse comes from understanding how it has damaged a witness for the name of Jesus Christ and caused others to stumble in their walk of faith.

Who Should Be Included in the Confession?

Confession should be made to God, to the spouse, and perhaps to others also. In the marriage, as confession is taking place, there should also be times when the offended spouse is able to hear the unfaithful spouse confess to the Lord in prayer. Genuine confession requires humble acknowledgement and apology. It also includes a request for forgiveness from the spouse.

> If we confess our sins, he is faithful and just and will forgive us our sins and purify us from all unrighteousness. (1 John 1:9)

The Bible teaches that we should confess our sins to God. He will forgive our sins and purify us from all unrighteousness. After confession, God promises to forgive us when we ask Him. The guilt has been removed because of God's grace. God's grace is wonderful and amazing. Accepting God's forgiveness is by faith, even though it is hard to fathom. Our trust is based on God's Word. Sometime we might wonder if God's forgiveness really applies to us. The answer is yes. We must confess as God instructed and then believe what He promised.

Who should one confess to? Confession should be to the people who have been sinned against. Some people may say you have sinned against everyone who knows you and is in any kind of relationship with you. Let's narrow the scope considerably. Typically, unfaithfulness in the marriage is a sin against the spouse and any children. Some may also include members of the spouse's family. A minister or a counselor can advise on what to confess to whom.

Confession to children needs to be handled very carefully and appropriately for each child. The child's age is an important consideration. Generally, the younger the child, the less specific facts needs to be confessed. The older the child, the more complete the confession may be. As children become older to late teens or adults and begin to ask more questions, perhaps more information can be given.

Confession to children should never be intended to blame them, scare them, blame the other parent, alienate them from a parent, or impel them to choose one parent over the other. Rather, the goal is to explain the appropriate information and to be redemptive and positive. Confession to children should always be done in ways that are truly in their best interest. It should not be done to incite anger or parental loyalty. The main focus is to waylay fears and anxieties and to remove any sense of responsibility or guilt the child may feel.

Early on, when the broken trust comes to light, there is a vast array of emotions. It is often difficult to manage the emotions without the children sensing something is wrong. Depending on their age, it may be appropriate for the unfaithful spouse to share with the children that he or she has made wrong choices and sinned against the other parent. This should only be done in the presence of the faithful spouse. It would be necessary to include the other parent in order to build trust and accountability.

Communicate a willingness to seek the Lord's guidance and trust in Him for strength and help. Assure the child of God's love and care for the family. Express unconditional love for the children and your devotion to them. Discuss how God gives strength in struggles, forgiveness for sins, and hope for the future. It is important to allow the children to express their feelings. Also, talking with another person like a trusted family member or minister may be very beneficial for the children.

Acknowledge, Apologize, Ask for Forgiveness

In relationships, whenever a person hurts another, taking specific meaningful steps is the best way to address the differences, resolve the conflict, and move forward to strengthen the relationship. These meaningful steps include going to that person and to each other to acknowledge the wrongs completely, apologize, and ask for forgiveness. Then with God's grace and forgiveness, hopefully, the conflict can be put in the past, and the relationship can move forward.

A simple formula for this can be remembered with three As.

- *Acknowledge* the sins and wrongs done. Be very specific. Complete confession is the first step to show sincerity in wanting to repent from the sins and hurtful actions and seek to rebuild trust with openness and honesty. At times in the process, spouses may wonder if there is real hope for their marriage to be restored. One of the biggest indicators of this is how willingly and completely the confession is done. After confession, as hard as it is to hear, most spouses through tears say, "Thank you for telling me the truth."

- *Apologize.* Express remorse for what you have done. After trust has been broken in a marriage, the most important words may be "I am very sorry. I will never do this again." Commit to repentance, which is changing your actions. Prove that you will not do the actions again. These promises seem inadequate and insignificant at this time. However, they can be a balm for the deep hurt the spouse is feeling and can be proven true with sincere follow-through.

- *Ask for forgiveness.* "Will you please forgive me?" Forgiveness is a gift. Ask for it humbly. We can forgive others because Jesus Christ has forgiven us. This is true for every believer and can be true for every person who wants to accept Jesus Christ as Savior and Lord.

All three parts are necessary. To acknowledge and apologize without asking for forgiveness feels as if there is no closure. If there is acknowledgement and a request for forgiveness but no apology, then it feels like "Where is the remorse?" If there is an apology and a request for forgiveness without specific acknowledgement, it may leave the impression that there is no ownership of personal wrongs done.

Acknowledgment of wrong, apologizing, and asking for forgiveness do not necessarily restore the trust or take away the pain. But these are important steps toward changed hearts and progress toward a renewed relationship. It is imperative for an offending spouse to confess sins that have harmed the marriage.

There needs to be a keen awareness of our holy God, who hates sin. He brings things to light and reveals wrongs. Many times a person may want to keep actions hidden or only partially confess. This is a very risky decision, because God makes things known. People are often shocked at circumstances that God allows to happen in order for the truth to come out.

Many times in my counseling office, I have thought, *I should take off my shoes because this is holy ground. Only God could do this.* I have been amazed at the lengths that God will go to powerfully and lovingly bring things to light. God pursues a person for confession, repentance, and a changed heart. Perhaps through job changes, neighbors speaking up, hacked dating websites, financial statements mailed, surveillance cameras, pictures on Facebook, and many other creative ways, God exposes sinful actions.

Do not wait for God to reveal things. His grace is immeasurable. He instructs truthfulness and honesty. He is righteous and holy and does not wink at sin. He loves people so much that He will do whatever is necessary to lay things bare and reveal the truth.

7

Severing Wrong Relationships

If a house is divided against itself, that house cannot stand.

—Mark 3:25

The Importance

How can a marriage grow stronger if there are distractions from other people or investments toward other relationships? The truth is, it cannot. This affirms why it is important to understand how and why to take appropriate steps to sever wrong, destructive, and distracting relationships. A divided mind results in a divided heart and a divided marriage.

> But when he asks, he must believe and not doubt, because he who doubts is like a wave of the sea, blown and tossed by the wind. That man should not think he will receive anything from the Lord; he is a double-minded man, unstable in all he does. (James 1:6–8)

A double-minded person hangs on to opposing goals or relationships. He is unstable, and he selfishly thinks that sin will bring happiness. The cheap substitute never comes close to the amazing joy of knowing and obeying God. A divided heart results in destruction. A marriage that seeks the Lord will be a lifelong blessing.

Sometimes as an affair becomes known, an unfaithful spouse may take the position, "I'm not sure which person I want to choose; I still love both." At that point, the choice is still for the affair, expecting the spouse to hang on and wait. This is an arrogant and hurtful attitude. The latter statement is untrue even when there is emotional attachment involved. Adultery is not based on true biblical love. God is love. The affair is self-serving. Nothing about the friendship or affair honors God.

As long as a spouse must be convinced of the merits of the marriage or of recommitting to it, the marriage cannot move forward. An unfaithful spouse may feel "empowered" by being persuaded or begged to stay. It is very unhealthy for a faithful spouse to be "willing to do anything" to keep the marriage. The wandering spouse may bargain and negotiate with an attitude of "How much do you want me?"

Sinful choices rip the heart of the committed spouse. Until the unfaithful spouse makes a definite and clear decision toward the Lord and away from destructive alternatives, there is no way for the marriage to be strengthened and reunited. The unfaithful spouse has completely lost sight of the vision of marriage as God designed it.

The allegiance must be to the marriage. If the appropriate priority had been on the marriage earlier, there would not have been another distracting relationship. Becoming involved in an extramarital relationship usually happens when guards are down. Bad choices are made. The solution is for the protections to be renewed and for appropriate decisions to be established.

The goal is to raise the marriage back to the position it ought to hold. The Bible teaches that the marriage is the priority relationship. God created and ordained marriage. It is sacred. He expects that we treat it as sacred. In the following verse, Jesus Christ was not commanding that eyes should be literally gouged out or hands cut off but rather that we must take serious steps in dealing with sinful actions and relationships.

> If your right eye causes you to sin, gouge it out and throw it away. It is better for you to lose one part of your body than for your whole body to be thrown into hell. And if your right hand causes you to sin, cut it off and throw it away. It is better for you to lose one part of your body than for your whole body to go into hell. (Matthew 5:29–30)

The Purpose

> Therefore, prepare your minds for action; be self-controlled; set your hope fully on the grace to be given you when Jesus Christ is revealed. As obedient children, do not conform to the evil desires you had when you lived in ignorance. But just as he who called you is holy, so be holy in all you do; for it is written: "Be holy, because I am holy." (1 Peter 1:13–16)

The purpose of taking intentional steps to remove damaging relationships is to separate from them to end the negative influence. Some may argue that it is acceptable to just ignore them. That is not sufficient when there has been unfaithfulness. Negative relationships generally do not "go away." There was deliberate agreement to enter the relationship, and it requires deliberate actions to end it.

Perhaps previous attempts seem to have been clear and definite but were not. Weeks, months, or years later, there may be a surprise contact from the past adulterous partner or alluring relationship. Hence, it is crucial to sever these relationships. The ability and accessibility for continued contact or influence must be eliminated.

The objective is to send a clear and unmistakable message that the wrong relationship will be completely and permanently ended. It is not to be continued or pursued in any way. No one can ever assume that the extramarital relationship will fade away and cease to be a problem. In fact, the opposite is usually true. Unless the relationship is completely dissolved, it is likely to recur.

The goal of severing a relationship is not to be punitive or retaliatory. Rather, it is to provide a fresh start and a hope for the marriage. Continuing to do everything the same way with just a little "tweaking" is not a viable solution. What is needed is complete termination of the wrong relationship. There should not be an option for reconnection or renewed communication in any way.

Developing a Plan

> The fear of the LORD is the beginning of wisdom,
> and the knowledge of the Holy One is
> understanding. (Proverbs 9:10)

Disconnection of a damaging relationship requires wisdom and commitment. The layers of issues that unfaithfulness produces can have a bearing on many people and cause many far-reaching effects. Caring about innocent people should be an emphasis. Handling the situation in ways to be "less hurtful" toward the adulterous partner is not the goal. Nor is it right to let the unfaithful spouse determine whether or how the situation is managed, though they often want to take charge.

> If any of you lacks wisdom, he should ask God,
> who gives generously to all without finding fault,
> and it will be given to him. (James 1:5)

This verse tells about how important it is to ask God for wisdom. Deciding the best ways to sever dangerous relationships requires wisdom. Wisdom is needed to know the best actions, timing, and methods. The wrong relationships cannot continue. They do not honor God. Appropriate fear of and reverence for God is the beginning of wisdom and the foundation for every good marriage.

The unfaithful spouse may feel there was no "closure" to the adultery. They often feel like they should "at least say good-bye." That is preposterous. The adulterous relationship is not only sinful but also adversarial to the marriage. The other person has participated with hostility to the marriage. The Bible teaches that we should flee temptation and deal decisively with sin.

Giving closure or saying good-bye is never a part of appropriate priorities and should not be the goal of a severance plan. The unfaithful relationship began with no consideration of the spouse. Ending that relationship should not be attuned to the unfaithful partner. Once the broken trust is found out, the unfaithful relationship must be stopped immediately. Severing it should permanently end all contact.

Many aspects need to be considered. The decisions are difficult. Not every situation or solution is the same. Some considerations are the length of the affair, how involved it was, and what needs to happen to end the connections and interfacing actions. Be aware of selfless-sounding options offered by the unfaithful spouse that in fact have an agenda for personal benefit.

End All Communication and Contact

Ending all communication in every way is the first and most important step in severing wrong relationships. This includes stopping all forms of social media, written, and verbal contacts and communications through other people. The married couple together should carefully delete all pertinent contact information. It needs to be done with both spouses present to build trust and accountability. There must be an accompanying promise to never reinstall the information anywhere.

Ending all contact means that the unfaithful spouse promises never under any circumstances to reach out or communicate to the outside person in any way. This additionally means a commitment not to respond in any way to the outside person who may try to communicate. Rather, if communications occur, the spouse must disclose this to the hurting spouse immediately. There should be no deleting, moving, or hiding it before showing it to the spouse. The faithful spouse can make a decision about what to do with it.

A godly counselor, minister, or neutral caring person can help both spouses discern the best way to accomplish this. The opinion of the faithful spouse and the helper should establish the steps and guidelines involved. The unfaithful spouse should be willing to defer to what they think is best. Hesitancy by the unfaithful spouse can be a red flag indicating a lack of repentance. A great deal about the heart of the wandering spouse is evident in how he or she follows through on definite plans.

Develop the Plan Together as a Couple

Every step should include both spouses and be done together in ways that strengthen the marriage and honor the faithful spouse above all others. Sometimes an unfaithful spouse may say, "I've already taken care of that" or "I'll be glad to take care of it, but want to do it in the way that I think is best." He or she may even add, "I want you to trust me with this." There is no reason to trust this spouse. He or she has been living in deception and lies and is untrustworthy at this time.

These statements are very inappropriate. The unfaithful spouse should not take any actions apart from the faithful spouse. Individual actions taken by an unfaithful spouse do not build trust and accountability or solve the problems. Instead, they are an excuse to have another contact with the other person. They harm the trust again.

Send a Severance Letter

One of the most effective methods for severing unfaithful relationships is to mail a severance letter. The note needs to be written together as a couple with a very concise and impersonal message and with no emotional descriptors. Type the note on plain white paper and mail in a plain white envelope. The unfaithful spouse should sign the note without handwriting anything else. The envelope should have no return address.

The note can say something like, "What we did was wrong. I will never communicate with you again. I will never contact you again. Do not ever contact me again in any way." The unfaithful spouse should sign the note, verifying who is actually sending it so the note will not look coerced by the spouse. Do not include greeting or closing statements or phrases. Both of the spouses need to be present to complete the letter and prepare it for mailing. The faithful spouse should be responsible for mailing it.

Most often, the address will be known and available. If not, it can usually be found on the Internet with current technology. Couples often choose to send it by certified mail because that requires a signature upon receipt. This gives the confidence that it has been received appropriately.

E-mails are not the best method. They are more personal with the information, and even the time is noted on the email. Also, e-mails can be forwarded to many people without anyone knowing. However, if e-mail is the only method, it is better than nothing at all. The communication to sever a relationship should not be done through a text message or a phone call or in person. All of these methods are personal, connect emotionally and invite a response.

The unfaithful spouse who is seeking to restore the marriage must commit to not having any contact with the outside partner in any way from now on. This certainly means not calling to warn of the arrival of the letter. If anything like this happens, it is clear that the spouse's heart remains unfaithful. These and other similar actions would go against any commitment to end the relationship and cease all contact in every way.

Often the argument is "What if a severance note ends up in the hands of someone who doesn't know?" or "What if it causes problems for the other marriage?" We can trust God's love and sovereignty for that other person and marriage as well. We can't see or know of the circumstances of the other couple, but God knows. We can trust God with the letter and any effects it has.

God wants all sin uncovered. He cares about both couples perfectly. God does not want unfaithfulness to be kept secret in any marriage. God is righteous. He is the holy and loving God. He desires the best for both couples. We can trust His love and control of the circumstances.

The letter can also serve as a catalyst in the other marriage for right actions to be taken. God can use it as a wake-up call to lovingly invite all involved to do right and stop the deception. We know God is working in the other marriage also, convicting their hearts of sin and drawing them toward truthful repentance.

When the Wrong Relationship Involves Someone Close

Close Friendships

Unfaithfulness involves situations that have layers of complications. The sad thing is that when disconnecting from relationships happens appropriately and completely, the innocent family members often pay a price and suffer in the process. Though heartbreaking, this may be necessary in order to assure the best chance for the marriage to be restored. The more directly an affair has involved familiar people and circumstances, the more painful it is for the faithful spouse and other family members.

The solutions are never easy but are essential. The temptation is to minimize what is necessary, gloss over the difficulties, or avoid making the tough decisions. The unfaithful spouse usually wants to do a minimal approach. Sometimes a spouse who was hurt by unfaithfulness in the marriage is hopeful for restoration and may say, "I guess we don't have to make huge changes" or "maybe I'm asking too much" regarding steps of severance.

There needs to be an advocate for that spouse who will say with wisdom and confidence, "No, you are not asking too much. Yes, these steps are absolutely necessary for restoring this marriage." If strong steps are not taken, the healing will be delayed or even blocked. Without the necessary methods of disconnecting, affairs often recur. They are just postponed or hidden until the opportunity presents itself. Renewed trust can be greatly delayed when that other person is still in the scope of regular life.

George and Kimberly were on rocky ground trying to determine whether their marriage was going to be reconcilable. George had just revealed to Kimberly that he had been in a relationship with one of her friends for several years. Kimberly was shocked and deeply hurt but wanted to save the marriage. George argued that the friendship could remain with "new boundaries" with the other person.

Kimberly wanted to "see the good in him and hope for the best." Sure enough, in a few weeks, George was back in the sinful relationship. Kimberly thought that though she really wanted a good marriage, any marriage with him was better than none at all. She settled for a marriage that included her husband continuing his adulterous relationship. This was not honoring to God.

Condoning sin is not showing grace or standing for what is right. George had become the idol of Kimberly's heart. Keeping him was more important than pleasing God. Doing what is right requires courage and faith. We cannot control the outcome or the choices of others. However, it is more important to trust God and draw the line on sin in a biblical way. Accepting unholy behaviors and relationships is wrong and contrary to God's principles.

Ellen Dean

Family Member

Unfaithfulness with an extended family member results in a very complicated situation. Prayerfully consider what to do about the relationship. Seek help from an objective, godly person. When an affair happens between relatives or close friends, the relationships will never be the same. To hope or imagine that eventually things can drift "back to normal" is not realistic and not fair to the deeply wounded spouse. Things must change drastically and permanently.

Sometimes a spouse commits adultery with in-laws or relationships by marriage. When this happens, there still needs to be a severing of the relationship in strong ways. It is not enough for the unfaithful spouse to promise not to do it again or to ignore the adulterous partner at gatherings of family or friends. Rather, the plan must include not being at the same place for family meals, holidays, reunions, sharing responsibilities with relatives, etc.

If the adulterous partner is not going to be present, the unfaithful spouse should be with the marriage partner. It causes apprehension and suspicions when the adultery partners are both absent from events. The only rare exceptions where both may be present would be for close family funerals or weddings at which they would stay visible to everyone and apart from each other.

At these times, the recommitted marriage partners need to work out a clear plan to avoid the wrong person and to protect trust. This means absolutely no communication with the other person and physically staying away from the other person. It also means staying close to the spouse at all times. Other pertinent family members need to be informed about the plan so they can be supportive.

Sadly, that other person's relationships not only with the faithful spouse but with children and other family member are affected also. Care and attentiveness to children's feelings help provide understanding and comfort during the difficult transitions and new situations. Family members may need counseling to process the changes and deal with all the resulting painful emotions. Attention and love should be given generously to innocent family members caught up as collateral damage.

Some extended family members may say, "Can't we just all ignore what's happened and get along?" "It's not fair that person can't come to the reunion" or "Is this really necessary?" The affair certainly wasn't fair to the hurting spouse. No one else has experienced what the offended spouse has felt. They can't fully empathize, nor should they be the decision makers. The person who has been sinned against is the person that family members should advocate for.

Vera learned that her husband, Harold, had been involved in an affair with her cousin. As Vera and Harold began to try to rebuild their marriage, she realized that it would be hard to continue both relationships. Harold was repentant and willing to make changes to become accountable and trustworthy. Vera chose to recommit to him, making the decision to not have an ongoing relationship with her cousin.

The choice would affect Vera greatly, but she was willing. She felt that the Lord was leading her to work to restore her marriage. Vera's family honored her decision and supported her. She felt their respect and encouragement. Now, years later, she knows she made the right decision. Her marriage has been restored.

Church Member

Sometimes affairs happen in churches. In these cases, the church staff and ministers need to be involved in decisions about how to sever the wrong relationships for the greatest healing. This may be difficult because no minister wants to lose people from leadership positions or families from the church membership. However, the most important priority needs to be on the rebuilding of the marriage units.

Both couples staying in the same church is not the best plan.

When a family goes to another church, the helping minister should ask for a permission statement to be signed by the couple so he can talk with the minister of the other church before new church membership is granted. This is to help set up accountability and a growth plan for the marriages involved.

The logical or sensible plan does not always win out. Sometimes one of the unfaithful spouses will exhibit a defiant attitude, resisting the wise counsel of the ministers, and refuse to go. This may be expressed as "This is my church too," "I was here first," or "We can both just stay, change classes, and worship in different services." This is a spiritually immature, insensitive, and unwise approach.

Usually the adultery partners want to have the greatest influence in developing the plan. However, the ones who should have the greatest input about the best solutions should be the spouses who have been hurt. Churches are keenly involved in trying to provide important help and ministry, with grace-filled options for all the spouses and both marriages.

It is very hard for couples to heal when they continue to remain at the same church after two of the spouses committed adultery. This may mean that ministers have to address the inconsideration and limited perspectives of the sinful partners who are trying to stay in the same circles, imagining that it should be acceptable for everyone. The same selfish hearts that drove the betrayal in the first place may try to determine a selfish minimal outcome.

Johnny and Chelsea served on a committee at church and began to meet sexually. When it came out, decisions had to be made. The church acted appropriately in behalf of the other spouses. The leaders' responses were biblical and grace-filled. One of the couples went to another church, and the ministers of both churches worked together to continue the discipline and ministry for the couples. Now both families are active in separate churches, and marriages are being restored.

When a woman was caught in adultery and brought to Jesus, the men expected Jesus to condemn her. Instead, Jesus bent down and wrote some things in the sand. We do not know what He wrote, but one by one all of the accusers left. She was standing alone with Jesus. He told her that He did not condemn her. She could leave and go to sin no more.

Jesus did not condone her sin but offered grace and forgiveness and the instruction to forsake the sin. In the same way, people should turn from sin and walk in righteousness. This means severing sinful relationships and walking in purity and holiness. Others should not condemn them.

> Jesus straightened up and asked her, "Woman, where are they? Has no one condemned you?"
>
> "No one, sir," she said.
>
> "Then neither do I condemn you," Jesus declared. "Go now and leave your life of sin." (John 8:10–11)

Someone in Close Proximity – Workplace, Neighborhood, Organization

Sometimes affairs happen between people who live in the same neighborhood or who work in the same place. In these circumstances extreme care needs to be applied in taking the appropriate steps to sever the unfaithful relationships. These situations can have tremendous impacts on family members, specifically those who were not involved in the destructive actions.

The decisions require evaluating whether a person needs to resign from a job, leave a workplace, drop out of an organization, change friendships, or even move to a different home. This brings tremendous grief and sadness for innocent family members. The negative consequences can be costly and inconvenient. They may uproot a family, cause an income reduction, or bring grief, discouragement, a sense of vicarious shame, and embarrassment. The ramifications can last for years.

Angela became aware of Carlton's sexual text messages to a coworker one night when she looked at his phone. She found an unknown phone number and messages that made her heart sink. Angela confronted Carlton. He was defensive and angry, responding with denial and minimization. He reluctantly agreed to go to counseling. Early in the process he lied about the extent of his actions and told Angela she needed to "stop making such a big deal about everything."

He ignored the heart issues and refused to acknowledge the huge breach of trust in the marriage. Soon he was engaging again in sexual messages with other women. Angela realized that she could not change his heart. She also knew that without repentance and a complete severance of bad relationships, unfaithful actions would continue. She could not expect that the trust would be restored in her marriage.

> We know that anyone born of God does not continue to sin …. (1 John 5:18)

Though one member of the marriage may have been the unfaithful one, it often seems as though everyone else pays with loss and adjustments. It doesn't seem fair, and it isn't fair. It takes faith to trust the Lord to bring good out of these difficult circumstances and to believe that He blesses people who make their marriage a priority. The Lord is honored when one acts in commitment to trust Him, live righteously, and seek to obey Him.

> And we know that in all things God works for the good of those who love him, who have been called according to his purpose. (Romans 8:28)

When life changes are necessary, to what degree should the details and reasons for these new decisions and changes be shared with some family members and others? How much disclosure and explanation are needed? These are important questions and should be carefully and thoughtfully discussed with a helping, godly, and objective person. The goal should be what helps and is best for the faithful and innocent family members, not the offending spouse.

Without information, it is hard to understand the difficult changes that must come. There needs to be enough revelation to explain the importance and necessity of these decisions. The unfaithful spouse should be willing to take responsibility for the upheaval. It should be the appropriate content and amount to be disclosed. That might include talking with family members, bosses, coworkers, and others as needed. This requires discretion and humility.

> And this is my prayer: that your love may abound more and more in knowledge and depth of insight, so that you may be able to discern what is best and may be pure and blameless until the day of Christ, filled with the fruit of righteousness that comes through Jesus Christ—to the glory and praise of God. (Philippians 1:9–11)

The ultimate focus needs to be on the discernment to know what is best. Decisions should center on the goal of being pure and blameless, filled with the fruit of righteousness to glorify God. Going forward in marriage and in family, the Lord and His leadership must be paramount. He is a loving, redemptive God and has wonderful plans to bless those who seek and follow Him.

8

Repentance and Heart Issues

I preached that they should repent and turn to God
and prove their repentance by their deeds.

—Acts 26:20

What Is Repentance?

What is repentance, and what does it look like in people's lives and
relationships? Repentance is described and defined as changing
directions. It means stopping negative behaviors and replacing them
with positive ones. Repentance is visible change in attitude and
action sustained over time. True repentance is more than just one
moment. It takes time and is distinctive, observable, and consistent.

Repentance is apparent when a person moves away from
destructive patterns and toward renewal and discipline. Over
time, a changed life shows measurable growth and meaningful
transformation. A remorseful person may say, "I'm sorry." A
repentant person says, "I'm sorry, and I won't do it again," and
then proves the words with permanently changed actions.

A genuine repentant heart shifts from a self-focused agenda
to honoring God and loving others. Selfish pride is replaced with
humility. A repentant heart is marked by an eagerness to change
and to do whatever it takes for as long as it takes to prove the

commitment to be trustworthy. True repentance appreciates the opportunity to acknowledge wrongs and wants to make amends. Repentance is absolutely essential for restoration.

An unrepentant heart focuses on self. It complains that the requirements are too hard or that too much is expected. It is insincere and plays the victim. False repentance wants to be begged and coerced. A person who is not sincerely repentant will protest, argue and attempt to negotiate.

Cameron and Molly were in relational upheaval. Molly was crashing emotionally. Recently, she had listened while Cameron confessed that he had been unfaithful with women for a long time. Though he said he would repent completely, soon he was backpedaling and hoping the confession was all that would be required. He hoped everything would be glossed over since he initiated the confession right before she found out. He didn't understand what real repentance is and what the Bible says is necessary.

> Produce fruit in keeping with repentance. (Matthew 3:8)

Contrasting Worldly Sorrow and Godly Sorrow

> Godly sorrow brings repentance that leads to salvation and leaves no regret, but worldly sorrow brings death. See what this godly sorrow has produced in you: what earnestness, what eagerness to clear yourselves, what indignation, what alarm, what longing, what concern, what readiness to see justice done. (2 Corinthians 7:10–11)

These verses contrast godly sorrow and worldly sorrow. There are radical differences. Godly sorrow has genuine grief, heartbroken about the choices made. This leads to changes in heart motives and behaviors. Without grief for sin and a commitment to turn life around, the sorrow is shallow regretting only about getting caught and having personal desires blocked.

Godly sorrow produces earnestness and truthfulness with genuine humility. It has an eagerness to clear oneself by developing a new and loving reputation. It expresses remorse with "I did a terrible offense to you." Alarm is the realization of harm done to someone else and is concerned for the other person's well-being. "I'm alarmed by the pain I've caused you." Godly sorrow understands there are consequences resulting from sins.

These attitudes accompany a deep longing to express guilt, sorrow, and shame resulting from the sin. Hope for a second chance depends on the realization that it is only possible by God's grace. Godly sorrow willingly enters a restoration process, patiently deferring to the offended spouse for what will be involved. "I am willing to do anything and everything that is necessary with no time limits in order to prove my faithful commitment to you. That includes even going to the counselor you choose for as frequently and as long as you think is needed."

Worldly sorrow is opposite of godly sorrow. Worldly sorrow impatiently focuses on self-protection and self-interest. It minimizes personal wrongs, cares more about personal reputation, wants an easy fix, blames others, and assumes that what is required will be excessive and unreasonable. Familiar questions are "What will repentance cost me? What will be involved, and how long will it take?"

Worldly sorrow is self-centered and says, "Can't we just move forward?" It is eager to clear oneself with the indignation of "I can't believe you are accusing me of that." "What are people going to think of me?" It short-circuits repentance with "Can't you just forgive me?" assuming forgiveness is all that is necessary.

Repentance Is Not the Only Component

True repentance involves more than just a desire to change direction in life. When someone really repents, they are different.

They want to have qualities that are honoring to God. Two characteristics produced by genuine repentance are a desire to restore trust and a desire to make things right. A truly repentant person will confirm these desires with actions.

Sometimes a spouse may claim to be repentant, insisting that everything will be okay. However, there may not have been adequate time or evidence for the other spouse to see real change. It is not so convincing for an offending spouse to declare personal repentance as for an offended spouse to witness the changes in clear and significant ways.

There are situations in which trust has been so severely broken that the offended spouse does not desire to continue in the marriage. Some hurting spouses may say, "Though there is repentance, I don't think I can ever trust you again." The answer requires seeking the Lord's will and direction. It will have an impact on many people for a long time.

If a marriage can be saved, it can be a huge blessing for the couple, for the children, for other family members, and for the name of our Lord. Even though God has provided biblical considerations regarding adultery, genuine repentance opens the possibility for restoration. Restoration should be the first plan of action if possible.

The Bible has a clear description of what takes place in a person's heart and life when one is sorry about sin and desires to do right and obey God. Ephesians 4:22–24 and Colossians 3:9–10 describe taking off of the old self and putting on the new self in Christ. This is a new path of righteousness, forsaking old sinful patterns, excuses, and actions. It brings new hope and confidence in relationships.

> You were taught, with regard to your former way
> of life, to put off your old self, which is being
> corrupted by its deceitful desires; to be made
> new in the attitude of your minds; and to put

on the new self, created to be like God in true
righteousness and holiness. (Ephesians 4:22-24)

Do not lie to each other, since you have taken off
your old self with its practices and have put on the
new self, which is being renewed in knowledge in
the image of its Creator. (Colossians 3:9–10)

Both of these passages first describe how someone without
Christ is filled with corrupt, deceitful, and selfish desires. Then
when one knows Jesus Christ, life is made new. This new life is
surrendered to God and filled with righteousness and holiness.
The Holy Spirit gives strength and wisdom to change and live in
a transformed way.

Characteristics of Repentance

Repentance is one of the most challenging parts of the restoration
process. Before someone can repent, he or she must radically
change the desire to indulge in deceptive behavior and replace it
with a sincere desire to obey God and do right. It requires dying to
self. Dying to self and personal desires is a result of "being crucified
with Christ."

I have been crucified with Christ and I no longer
live, but Christ lives in me. The life I now live in
the body, I live by faith in the Son of God, who
loved me and gave himself for me. (Galatians 2:20)

Dying to self does not happen by ease or by our own strength.
It takes place by surrendering in faith to Jesus Christ, who died for
us because He loves us. Repentance is turning from past sins and
turning to God and His righteousness. God strengthens a person
who walks in faith, trusting Him.

> And without faith it is impossible to please God,
> because anyone who comes to him must believe
> that he exists and that he rewards those who
> earnestly seek him. (Hebrews 11:6)

Repentance is a paradigm shift. It's a switch from living sinfully to living righteously; from hiding to transparency; from pulling away to connecting; from disregarding to acting with love; from minimizing sin to seeing it as God sees it; from procrastinating to dealing with issues; from being lazy to being motivated; and from being mean to being kind.

Hunter had been unfaithful in some of the most extreme ways. Lucy was completely devastated. Hunter said he wanted to recommit to their marriage and become trustworthy again. There was not much hope from a human perspective. Hunter committed to repent and began to spend time in prayer and reading the Bible. Gradually at first, then more and more as time went on, a transformation began to take place in his heart, his attitude, and his actions. God began to tenderly heal Lucy's heart.

This was possible only with the power of the Holy Spirit and Hunter's surrendering his heart. Hunter's arrogant pride melted away. His defining selfishness changed to sacrificial love for others. His impatience and excuses were replaced by calmness and transparency. His lust for material things changed to focus less on his image and impressing others and more on honoring God with their resources. Today their marriage is restored, and they are actively serving the Lord.

Thomas and Sally have a different story. Sally was unfaithful in the marriage. She was resistant to humbling her heart and not willing to look at her actions and motives. How dare anyone confront her and ask her to realize the impact of her sins on others? Over time it became clear that Sally was not going to acknowledge her sins or repent. Thomas was heartbroken, and the marriage remained shattered.

Repentance is a turning from sin and turning toward God

and righteousness. A person cannot keep one foot on each side. A person is either seeking the Lord or living for self. Repentance is abandoning former wrong behaviors and wanting to live a righteous life. Other people can see the difference. Repentance is being broken about sin and choosing a fresh, new start all at the same time.

Repentance is trusting God. It is counterintuitive to the normal human response. It ceases to defend and justify sinful actions. Repentance wants to abandon pride and desires to love God. It is deeper than just wanting to save a marriage. It is radically different than "just forgive and move on." It cares about how things impact others. Sincere grief for past wrong actions transforms to a longing to strengthen the trust and rebuild what has been devastated.

Grace is not condoning sin or overlooking spiritual rebellion. In fact, it is love so compelling, tender, and undeserved that it can powerfully draw a heart like a magnet. Kindness can be quite persuasive in encouraging repentance. A beautiful picture of God's grace toward us is Romans 2:4:

> Or do you show contempt for the riches of his kindness, tolerance and patience, not realizing that God's kindness leads you toward repentance?

Alex and Carmen had been happily married for eleven years when she began to explore Facebook. Before long a guy from her small high school contacted her. She was delighted to connect with someone from the past. Very soon, naively and without appropriate caution, she began to dialogue with him more and more.

Carmen talked with Alex about the contact, but he was nonchalant and unconcerned. The conversations and contacts became more frequent and began to take on a different and sexual tone. At first, she discounted them and convinced herself that surely that was not what he meant. He had always been a nice guy. She was blindsided by his overtures.

When it dawned on her that she had been reckless and vulnerable, she stopped all contact and told Alex everything. Nothing more had happened between her and the high school friend. She was open, honest, and remorseful as she confessed. She apologized to Alex for not being careful about the conversations. She asked for his forgiveness. Alex responded with gentleness and grace.

Alex acknowledged his lack of appropriate concern and apologized for not being protective and discerning. He realized his minimal involvement made her more vulnerable to the illicit conversations. Both acknowledged the need to repent and focus on strengthening their marriage. They declared their love for each other and asked for forgiveness. Alex contacted the guy and asked him not to contact Carmen again. They both chose to get off Facebook and other social media sites.

Restitution is another dimension of repentance. Many times after wrong actions have occurred, there is a desire and a need to make things right toward those who have been affected. Sins cannot be erased, but efforts can be made to acknowledge them and in tangible ways to correct what can be corrected. Some examples could be to replace a borrowed tool that had been broken or lost, to repair scratches on a car from irresponsible actions, or to buy a gift to signify a change of heart.

> But Zacchaeus stood up and said to the Lord, "Look, Lord! Here and now I give half of my possessions to the poor, and if I have cheated anybody out of anything, I will pay back four times the amount." (Luke 19:8)

A biblical example for repentance and restitution is Zacchaeus. When Jesus went to Zacchaeus's house, he realized that Jesus was the Messiah. He put his faith in Jesus Christ and became a follower. Zacchaeus acknowledged his sin and wrongdoing as a tax collector. He made a commitment to repent and completely change his actions. He committed to give half of his possessions to the poor and to repay four times any amount he had stolen from people. The Lord did not say, "Oh, that's not necessary." Instead Jesus allowed him to make that commitment.

Repentance is stopping old sinful patterns and beginning good behaviors. The Bible teaches that a person honors God by choosing to do right even when it is hard. People are blessed as they turn in repentance to trust the Lord. Lives and relationships are changed profoundly and miraculously when a person responds to God's biblical guidelines and direction.

Red Flags Regarding Lack of Repentance

The spouse who broke the trust often wants shortcuts, becomes defensive, rewrites history, makes excuses, deflects issues, and bargains or negotiates. All of these reveal a lack of repentance.

Sullen and Self-Focused

Deidra was striving to rebuild the marriage after Paul's affairs. He had stopped his unfaithfulness but was not repenting in other ways. Instead he would escape into silence and sullen moods when he didn't get constant attention and affection from her. He was uncaring about how brokenhearted she was because of his unfaithfulness.

He had actively pursued his adulterous partners but expected Diedra to always pursue him. He wanted Deidra to be so glad to have him back that she would strive to fill his bottomless pit of selfish cravings. Deidra was a treasure, but he failed to value and respect her. He did not care about her needs and desires.

Unwilling to Discuss Issues and Establish Hedges

Charles became convicted by the Holy Spirit to confess his unfaithfulness. He wanted to get it off his chest. Heather was understandably shocked and crushed. After confession, Charles thought, *The worst is over*, and he hunkered down to get through the rest of the restoration process. He didn't want to talk about it because "it makes me feel uncomfortable and on the hot seat." He was reluctant to make changes in his job and relationships that had been "too friendly." He sought to shortcut the process, arguing that changes were too hard.

Refusal and Sabotage

A heart of rebellion resists repentance. The noncompliant spouse needs to be confronted. That can reveal many selfish complaints and frustrations. The unwilling spouse makes excuses and challenges guidelines. "This is crazy and unreasonable." "Why am I the only one who has to make changes?" "No matter what I do, it will not be enough."

Grace had been unfaithful to Bentley. She expressed a desire to commit to the marriage but refused to take meaningful steps of rebuilding accountability. She felt like counseling was an imposition and a distraction from her busy socialite schedule. She thought that Bentley should immediately put her affair behind them and take steps to prove his love to her by purchasing a new and larger home as she requested.

Sometimes the faithful spouse is the one who sabotages the appropriate actions. Blake had been unfaithful and verbally abusive to Jennifer. He was arrogant and disrespectful. He thought his wrong behaviors were not a big deal. When others tried to confront him, she minimized his actions, and he continued the destructive ways of disregarding her. She said she cared more about keeping his big salary than she cared about having his respect.

What if There Is No Repentance?

God hates unfaithfulness. The Holy Spirit convicts a spouse of the sinfulness of the actions. Hopefully, the unfaithful spouse will be drawn toward confession, repentance, and significant life transformation. It will be revealed over time whether there is real repentance.

If not, God will reveal that too. Pray, asking God for wisdom and discernment. Patiently seek the Lord, waiting for Him to lead and guide. He will give direction, clarity, and peace in your heart for the right decisions and actions.

Seek guidance and counsel from the Bible and from wise, godly, objective people to walk through this time with you. People in the world will offer opinions and answers. Be discerning, and evaluate them based on biblical truth. It is imperative not to make hasty decisions about the future.

> Trust in the LORD with all your heart
>   and lean not on your own understanding;
> in all your ways acknowledge Him,
>   and He will make your paths straight.
> (Proverbs 3:5–6)

It is necessary to trust almighty God, who knows all things about the future and the hearts of people. All decisions made should obey God and be attentive to His leading and guiding in the situation. It is vital to appropriately address all significant issues. When children are part of the picture, they naturally bring extra concerns. The problems need to be considered in the present, but a long look forward is required as well.

True repentance is an essential key to healing and restoration in marriage. It begins with completely acknowledging the sinful actions that broke the trust in the marriage. Next is surrendering to Jesus Christ in all actions and attitudes. Repentance is revealed in the heart of an individual who wants to then strive to prove an authentic, trustworthy change.

Repentance is moving from transgressions to holiness, faithfulness, and purity. The primary focus is the desire to honor and obey God. The most important goal is not to save a marriage but to walk humbly, holy, and obedient before the Lord Jesus Christ. The benefits and blessings are very impactful for the individual, the marriage, and the family relationships.

9

Understanding the Emotions and Responses

> Therefore, as God's chosen people, holy and
> dearly loved, clothe yourselves with compassion,
> kindness, humility, gentleness and patience.
> (Colossians 3:12)

Broken trust in a marriage brings a wide spectrum of emotions for both spouses. Discussing the emotions brings greater understanding and hope for healing. Understanding these emotions and learning how to express and process them is crucial. This often requires an objective person to help facilitate wisely and compassionately.

There are emotions that are unique to the offended spouse and others that are unique to the offending spouse. Others may be common to both. It's difficult to understand all the emotions. It is important to give attention to what is right and best, or else emotions can give way to impetuous decisions that can cause harm.

Helping in a Sensitive Way

Minimizing emotions does not feel caring. Focusing only on emotions can impede healthy progress. The right balance helps insure movement toward healing. One spouse feels devastated by the actions of broken trust. The spouse who broke the trust is faced with the aftermath. Those helping can connect authentically and offer objectivity.

The guiding principles for processing emotions should be based on God's Word. Situations are complicated; human wisdom and personal views are inadequate to lead individuals and the marriage to the most positive outcomes. There is much at stake, so wisdom from God is needed. It is necessary to ask God for wisdom, and He will give it.

> If any of you lacks wisdom, he should ask God,
> who gives generously to all without finding fault,
> and it will be given to him. (James 1:5)

Unexpected Responses

A remarkably frequent experience occurs shortly after broken trust is revealed. When the offending spouse acknowledges, confesses, expresses remorse, and commits to repentance, surprisingly, a honeymoon-like euphoria often follows for the couple. The couple feels closer than they have in a long time, hopeful and optimistic about a fresh start. Many times this transpires even before significant changes have been made.

This new feeling of closeness is relief that the spouse has "returned" and the marriage is not lost. The wounded spouse, desiring to make things easy for the unfaithful partner, becomes the protector, determined to prevent the spouse from leaving. Attempting to reconcile as quickly as possible sabotages the necessary work to be done for real confession and repentance.

Minimizing confrontation and avoiding painful discussions may accommodate and pacify the offending spouse, but it harms the hurting spouse. It does not strengthen a marriage. Rather, it helps a person ignore the conviction from the Holy Spirit. This diminishes the greatest potential for growth and change.

Counterintuitive, Meaningful Responses

When a spouse breaks the trust in marriage, it causes immense and long-lasting pain. The offending spouse needs to understand that it hurts deeper and longer than one can imagine. The faithful spouse wonders, "Does he still remember I am hurting?" When the offending spouse acknowledges the wrongs done and apologizes, even though he has already apologized before, the hurting spouse feels cared for.

A response from the offending spouse that helps the offended spouse is to intentionally and often say, "I haven't forgotten how much I have hurt you. I am very sorry." This shows humility and love. This one gesture has some of the most powerful impact toward emotional healing. Express authentic remorse until the hurting spouse says, "You don't have to continue to say that regularly now. But I'm thankful that you remember my pain." The hurting spouse will be thankful for all the expressions of remorse and regret.

An offending spouse's reactions can either help the healing or cause continued pain for the hurting spouse. These have a huge impact on how soon the hurting spouse can move forward emotionally. With real repentance, the sinful spouse is grieved that he has been so terribly selfish and destructive to the marriage. The hurting spouse should be the one to determine the time when "We can move forward now."

Conversely, to the degree the attitude of the offending spouse denies or minimizes the sins committed and avoids doing what is necessary because of a prideful heart, the process of marital healing is extremely limited. "I've already apologized. Isn't that enough?" This is not the right response. It is also important for the hurting spouse to be willing to hear the acknowledgment and regret expressed by the offending spouse. Ignoring, minimizing, or dismissing it is not appropriate or helpful and delays healing and forgiveness.

Wrong Responses by the Offended Spouse

Sometimes in frustration, especially in cases of unfaithfulness, the faithful spouse will say, "Just go to the other person since you want to be there so much. Go ahead and go!" These statements give apparent approval or excuse for the unfaithful spouse to continue in sinful behavior. Though an expression of pain, the statements are still inappropriate. We are never to entice or encourage someone toward sin.

Incongruent messages are confusing. The hurting spouse does not really want the other spouse to continue in adultery. Rather, the desire is for the adultery to be replaced with renewed commitment to the marriage. In extreme anguish one may say illogical and incorrect statements. These are detrimental and cause additional problems.

It is not beneficial for a hurting spouse to quickly say, "I forgive you," before there has been confession and acknowledgement. The desire for closeness often rushes into premature reconciliation. Definitely, the decision to forgive needs to be part of the process and is not optional. However, at this point in the process it could seem to give the offending spouse a pass to be off the hook for the transformational work that needs to be done by the Holy Spirit.

Another inappropriate response to hurting emotions is to seek revenge or threaten to harm anyone. Even when huge injustices have been committed, only behaviors that are honoring to God are acceptable. God, our righteous Lord, deals with sin. We cannot.

Stay the course with self-control. Do not choose actions that bring regret. Commit to do what is right regardless of what someone else does or doesn't do. Focus on the issues that need to be addressed. Trust God, who is our defender, to handle the accounting. God sees and knows, and He is able to deal with transgressions. There is nothing gained in retaliation.

> Do not take revenge, my dear friends, but leave
> room for God's wrath, for it is written: "It is mine

to avenge; I will repay," says the Lord. (Romans 12:19)

Do not be deceived: God cannot be mocked. A man reaps what he sows. The one who sows to please his sinful nature, from that nature will reap destruction; the one who sows to please the Spirit, from the Spirit will reap eternal life. Let us not become weary in doing good, for at the proper time we will reap a harvest if we do not give up. (Galatians 6:7–9)

Wrong Responses by the Offending Spouse

There are several common wrong responses by the offending spouse. It is selfish and unkind to gloss over one's own sins and try to move forward too quickly. With real repentance, the sinful spouse does not promote "Can we just move forward?" The hurting spouse should be the one to determine the time of moving forward.

The spouse who has caused the hurtful circumstances should not criticize a hurting spouse's emotional responses of sadness and anger. This hypocritical lack of introspection is arrogant and insensitive. The offending spouse should remember his own shortcomings and not critique the emotions of the hurting spouse.

An offending spouse saying, "Why do you have to be so angry?" "Why do you cry so much?" "It's too hard on me when you're upset like this," or "You are supposed to forgive me" are poor attempts to minimize personal culpability, blame the other, and play the victim. The selfish spouse was willing to do immeasurably hurtful actions toward the other spouse and now is piously pointing fingers.

Handling emotions tenderly and lovingly is long overdue. Spouses who break the trust in their marriage should be humble and caring toward the hurting spouse. Take personal responsibility. Acknowledge that the actions done against the marriage are the reasons for the unfathomable emotional pain and sorrow felt by the spouse. Commit to care more about the marriage partner. Realize that it is because of the spouse's grace that you are still in the relationship.

Cindy was the main breadwinner for the family, the responsible one, caregiver for the children, managing the home and putting others' needs above her own. Often she felt overwhelmed and asked Larry for help, but he refused. He did the minimal, expected lots of praise, wanted to be the center of attention, avoided tough jobs and did not want any accountability.

Then Larry had an affair. Now he pouts, shuts down, and walks out when Cindy cries or gets upset because of the affair. "You're always crying," Larry says. "I'm not going to talk to you when you're upset." He is self-righteous and controlling. Consistently, the focus is on his self-consumed desires. Cindy feels discouraged and hopeless. She realizes that Larry's disregard of her has been present throughout the marriage.

The Offended Spouse's Emotions

Shock ... or Not

It is a shock for a spouse to find out that his or her spouse has done something that breaks the trust in the marriage. Even with earlier suspicions, to finally know the facts is alarming. As more facts trickle out, the news feels surreal, and the deep emotional pain increases.

In some cases, there is not so much shock. Instead, there are feelings of "I'm not surprised. I've suspected this." The broken trust may be expected because there has been a pattern of questionable behaviors and lack of accountability.

In shock, thoughts are whirling. Decisions and response mechanisms are at a standstill. The rest of life is a blur. This is similar to finding out that a loved one has died suddenly. There are immediate needs and responsibilities. These individuals may do uncharacteristic actions and need support to take one step at a time through the first minutes, hours, and days.

Carlie heard that her husband had an affair. In shock she forgot to pick up their child from school. Donna mindlessly drove to a nearby town and checked into a hotel. Susan sat for hours in her car in a park until a police officer escorted her home. All were surprised by their own behavior.

When one is reeling emotionally, good judgment does not always prevail. Grant learned that his wife had left town with another man. He finished his golf outing and had hot dogs with his buddies before going home. When he arrived home, he realized that family members had stepped in to help with the crisis.

> Have mercy on me, O God, have mercy on me,
>   for in you my soul takes refuge.
> I will take refuge in the shadow of your wings
>   until the disaster has passed. (Psalm 57:1)

Grief

Grief is a strong emotion. Deep sadness crashes over, knocking the emotional footings out from under a spouse. Grief is overwhelming sadness about all that has transpired to possibly destroy the marriage.

It can come in waves, a hopeless and debilitating feeling. A faithful spouse's heart can be so wounded that it closes down. "My feelings died then." "My heart is numb." These are statements of terrible pain.

Grief often continues through the restoration process. It is felt when driving by places where a spouse has been unfaithful or in parts of town where the marriage was touched by sin. An unfaithful spouse needs to be aware that the grief their spouse feels lingers for a long time.

Family members and friends can help. Validate the grief, but encourage the hurting spouse to process it appropriately. This happens by choosing right actions even when there doesn't seem to be the emotional energy to do it. A person can "stall out" if he or she doesn't have healthy motivation and support.

The hurting spouse, focusing on the pain and the injustice, says, "This is not how it is supposed to be. I didn't sign up for this." The most important help in times of grief is from the Lord and His Word. The Bible is full of passages describing God's presence and comfort. We are instructed to intentionally give our sorrows to the Lord.

> Cast your cares on the Lord
>   and he will sustain you;
> he will never let
>   the righteous be shaken. (Psalm 55:22)

> The righteous cry out, and the Lord hears them;
>   he delivers them from all their troubles.
> The Lord is close to the brokenhearted
>   and saves those who are crushed in spirit.
>   (Psalm 34:17–18)

Sydney was filled with grief when she found out about Tom's lies and wrong behaviors. She never drank before but chose to go to a neighborhood bar and drink away her pain. The establishment manager called her sister to come and pick her up. The next morning, she realized that her remedy for the pain only complicated her life, shifting the focus off Tom's behavior to her own. She was filled with regret and humiliation, and the pain was still there. She committed to finding a better option for dealing with her feelings.

Anger

Anger is a common and understandable emotion after trust is broken in marriage. Anger proclaims that an injustice has been committed. Anger is either righteous or unrighteous. Righteous anger is outrage about things that God is angry about. Even righteous anger can quickly become unrighteous if expressed wrongly. Self-control needs to be in place to handle anger in a positive way when one is tempted otherwise. For the hurting spouse to feel anger is reasonable and understandable, but it should be expressed appropriately, in a controlled and productive way.

> My dear brothers, take note of this: Everyone should be quick to listen, slow to speak and slow to become angry, for man's anger does not bring about the righteous life that God desires. (James 1:19–20)

Anger can produce many complications if not kept in check. Knee-jerk reactions cause more problems and rarely end well. Anger unleashed is not acceptable, and the results cannot be undone. Pause, seek counsel, and avoid any words or actions that can harm others and later produce personal consequences.

Spouses who vent their anger improperly cannot justify their own extreme actions. Vengeful behaviors such as stalking, threatening, contacting others randomly, sending accusing messages, and using social media to attack and belittle are wrong and possibly even illegal.

Even when sinned against, one's motivations need to honor God and act lovingly to others. Caution is needed to avoid future regrets or miscalculations. One sin does not justify another sin. Use self-control and wisdom to handle anger appropriately.

> In your anger do not sin. (Ephesians 4:26)

Sometimes the offended spouse imagines what he or she would like to say if faced with the unfaithful spouse's adultery partners. On some occasions there may be an appropriate time for these actions. However, this needs careful thought, prayer, and discussion with an objective person with biblical wisdom. Any actions should be delayed and only be done in ways and for reasons that honor God and would have a positive outcome.

Zelda was very angry about Mitchell having an affair with a neighbor. Her initial reactions were to tell their children about "Daddy's sin" followed by telling several others. Then she allowed her children to see her rage by tearing up pictures and throwing them all over the house. These actions were inappropriate and detrimental to any positive steps of dealing with the crisis.

Rejection

Broken trust in a marriage produces feelings of rejection. Being abandoned and "replaced" feels like being tossed aside, worthless. Feelings of rejection can change the confidence of a spouse and diminish feelings of being valued. Unless addressed, these feelings of being spurned can permeate a spouse's sense of significance. It is important to remember that one's value is in Jesus Christ. Continue to be the best you can be.

God gives people worth. He created each person and died for them. No one can take that away. When a person feels rejected, it's easy to doubt God's love. The one who should be the most loving has caused much pain instead. When a person is experiencing feelings of rejection because of sinful spousal actions, a kind person can help redirect their thinking back to how much God loves them. God's love never changes.

Rejection involves sad feelings of comparison and "not measuring up". Many times a spouse will think, *I must not have been enough, since my spouse was unfaithful.* Unfaithfulness has nothing to do with whether a spouse was good enough. Though an unfaithful spouse may try to blame the other spouse, when someone breaks marital trust, it is about that person willfully choosing to sin.

Also, the offended spouse commonly reports, "I feel like a fool." This spouse is not the fool. The foolish one is the one who thinks he or she can get away with sinful actions that dishonor God and hurt others. Most of the time, the faithful spouse has previously noticed red flags, asked questions, and received only lies. Hearing facts can actually prove they were right about the previous concerns and suspicions.

Fear and Confusion

Actions that break the trust in marriage cause feelings of fear and confusion in the other spouse. Suddenly things that felt secure and confident become precarious and unreliable. What was thought to be trustworthy has become dishonest and self-serving. Uncertainties and shifting situations make it difficult to understand what is steadfast. Promises and previous commitments seem to have been thrown away.

The confusion about the reasons and questions about why may never be completely answered. It is better to focus on other areas that can be sorted out. Fear sets in regarding the future. Take one step at a time. The ups and downs of the concerns following a marital breach of trust can divert you to a discouraging detour. Seek the Lord during this time of uncertainty. He will guide you step by step.

> Whether you turn to the right or to the left, your
> ears will hear a voice behind you, saying, "This is
> the way; walk in it." (Isaiah 30:21)

God is our strength and helps each one who seeks Him. He loves you. God does not wink at sin or ignore it. He is the righteous, sovereign Lord. Pray for wisdom, and He will give it generously. God brings clarity and direction when we ask Him to guide. Give Him your concerns and questions, and He will comfort you. Read the Bible daily and pray. Prayer is amazing. It is talking to God at any time about anything.

> For I am the Lord, your God,
>   who takes hold of your right hand
> and says to you, Do not fear;
>   I will help you. (Isaiah 41:13)

Depression

"Immersed in pain." Grief and anger can notch up to depression and begin to diminish motivation and emotional fortitude. Depression stifles functionality and productivity. When depression sets in, a person may need to be monitored more closely by loved ones and biblical helpers because hopelessness can take root. This leads to extreme discouragement, even suicidal ideations. If you hear someone express these extreme emotions, do not minimize the concern. Walk alongside, and bring in reinforcements as needed.

The overwhelming spectrum of emotional pain and frustration can threaten a person's ability to respond wisely and with good judgment. Be aware if the hurting person is pulling away, isolating, and avoiding responsibilities. The best remedy for depression is to choose willfully to take steps for right actions even if the emotions don't agree. If you are the hurting spouse, please seek help. Tell how you are feeling, and be open to counseling and encouragement.

Sandra was devastated when her husband, Michael, was unfaithful with his coworker. The depression became so severe that she began to contemplate and talk about the possibility of suicide. Family and friends rallied around her, offering hope and encouragement. She began to gain a more positive perspective by shifting her source of hope from Michael's behavior and decisions back to trusting God and His plan for her life. This empowered her to address Michael with appropriate resolve and personal strength.

> Why are you downcast, O my soul?
>> Why so disturbed within me?
> Put your hope in God,
>> for I will yet praise him,
>>> my Savior and my God. (Psalm 42:5)

Shame

Shame feels like the world is staring back in disdain. Spouses feel it when the trust has been broken in their marriage. Shame feels like being broken and damaged. Interestingly, the spouse who broke the marital trust may not feel shame at all and have no trouble justifying or minimizing personal transgressions.

A difficult aspect of shame is what I call "vicarious shame." This is when someone bears the shame for another person's wrongdoing. The person to whom the violation was directed is probably more aware personally of right and wrong. This moral compass leads to feelings of disgust at what has transpired and awareness of how others may view the indiscretions.

An example of vicarious shame is a six-year-old boy who wakes himself up, climbs out of bed, splashes water on his face, and goes to the pile of clothes on the floor looking for his little blue school shirt. He lays it on his bed and tries to rub out the wrinkles. Then he puts it on, buttoning it crookedly, but doing his best. He goes to the kitchen, glancing sideways to see his parents still laid out on the chair and sofa in the den; they haven't moved since their drunken stupor the night before.

Finding a loaf of bread, a dirty knife, and an open peanut butter jar, he dips some out and clumsily spreads it on the bread. Then he squishes the two pieces of bread together and stuffs it into his lunchbox. Grabbing his little jacket, he goes out the front door to meet the bus, where he ducks away from smirks and hears comments from older students making fun of how unkempt he looks.

He finally arrives at the school and goes into his classroom, embarrassed about his appearance and humiliated by the perceived shame. Thank the Lord for his sweet teacher, who greets him kindly and quietly asks if she can help him straighten out his shirt buttons. He nods with his head down. Then he sits in his chair trying to ignore the stares of classmates. The shame he feels because of his parents' selfishness, irresponsibility, and neglect floods over his life. In the same way, when a marriage partner commits terrible acts, the shame permeates the faithful spouse.

> Fixing our eyes on Jesus, the pioneer and perfecter of our faith. For the joy set before him endured the cross, scorning its shame, and sat down at the right hand of the throne of God. Consider him who endured such opposition from sinners, so that you will not grow weary and lose heart. (Hebrews 12:2–3)

This very meaningful passage of scripture speaks of how Jesus Christ faced shame and scorn on our behalf. This helps us realize that when we experience shame, Jesus understands and comforts.

> Those who look to him are radiant;
>> their faces are never covered with shame.
> (Psalm 34:5)

Bitterness

Anger, rejection, and disappointment fill a person's heart after unfaithfulness or other causes of broken trust in marriage. They feel all-consuming. These emotions can ferment into bitterness if not checked. Bitterness harms the person who was hurt more than the person who sinned. It grows larger in a wounded heart.

A faithful spouse feels bitterness and resentment because of increased responsibilities and home management tasks when the other spouse is acting irresponsibly. The faithful spouse has to take care of everything at the same time that he or she is trying to manage turbulent emotions. Things crash down around the hurting spouse, while the offending spouse appears to suffer minimal consequences.

Many times when unfaithfulness ravages a marriage, the faithful spouse might say, "I have always been here doing the responsible things for our family, while my spouse was absent and uncaring. Now I am hurting desperately, and I am expected to just move forward. It's not fair. Earlier my spouse was selfish and irresponsible, and everything fell on me. I had the hardest job before and have the hardest job now, too."

The Bible teaches us to let go of bitterness and to trust God, as hard as that seems. We can absolutely know that the Lord acts according to His righteousness and for our good. Many people either have not chosen or have not been taught to rely on God's faithfulness. However, choosing to trust God and be obedient to Him brings grace and power in life. God comforts hearts and gives wisdom for decisions and strength to handle responsibilities.

> Get rid of all bitterness, rage and anger, brawling and slander, along with every form of malice.
> (Ephesians 4:31)

Emotional Dilemma

Many people who have been deeply hurt because of marital unfaithfulness describe an early difficult emotional dilemma. This dilemma is the confusion about decisions and expectations for the future. The spouse believed the marriage would always be trustworthy and certain. Then the terrible news came out. Hopes and dreams were shattered. The story got worse as details became known.

The faithful spouse has to deal with the rejection, crushing emotions and compounding grief. She is crashing emotionally and searching her heart and faith for answers and directions. Nothing seems predictable anymore. The future is full of uncertainties, confusion, and sorrow. She is in no state to clearly and wisely think through options for the future yet, though others may be encouraging an immediate reaction.

Her husband has said that he is sorry about the affair and wants to reconcile the marriage. It seems that since he confessed, he is feeling better and hopeful for the future and has barely missed a beat in the rhythm of life. She loves him but hates his sinful actions. She feels as though nothing has been sorted through yet. She feels that no one truly understands her anguish. Instead, some seem to encourage her to accept his remorse at face value, and others want her to make a rash decision. Neither is right.

A hurting wife wonders about her husband's sincerity and whether she can ever trust him again. She hopes he'll truly repent but also knows personally the impacts of his selfish heart. Desperately she wants to believe in the new change and apparent fresh start in the marriage yet knows the real proof will be later in coming. She's right, and it may be later than she understands now. It is important to slow things down and not take any immediate actions regarding the future.

The emotional conflict is often between wanting to be separate from him because of the emotional devastation and also wanting to be with him because of love for him. As he shows new characteristics of spiritual renewal, she wants to believe their marriage and family will be different, more godly, honest, and loving. But the sins he shrugged off with confession have been dumped on her in crushing emotional blows. She needs time to observe his changed life.

The dilemma is dealing with present hurt and the future uncertainty with or without him. Remembering all that has transpired, she wishes she could expel him and not to have to continue in the anguish and turmoil. Yet she knows that if his heart truly changes, he may become more Christlike, walking closely with the Lord. He could become the husband she has always wanted and yearned for in their marriage.

If she rejects him, he will very likely remarry, even though he does not have biblical grounds to do so. "Someone else will have the blessing of him being different, without all the hurt and heartbreak that I have had to deal with." The emotional confusion should not give in to a quick fix or an initial decision. Proving a changed heart and life takes time. She needs to process her emotions before any decisions are made about the future.

Seeing his new godliness and attentiveness may be a double sadness. The hurt from the damaged marriage seems unbearable, yet possibly losing the marriage is heart-wrenching, fearful, and uncertain. The hurt spouse often says, "I miss out on both accounts: to stay married after being hurt so badly and hope things get better, or to divorce him and miss out on possible changes. He seems to have an easy pass. He gets blessings either way. I am suffering indescribably."

These emotions are understandable but miss some important aspects about how God deals with sin and about the steps to take after unfaithfulness has been found out. Also, they are thought processes that are premature and based only on the unfaithfulness and initial feelings. These considerations can come later after praying, sorting carefully through emotions, and giving the spouse an opportunity to show genuine repentance.

This reactive reasoning first assumes that the faithful spouse is the only spouse who is hurt by the unfaithfulness. This is not accurate. Sin destroys. It harms all who are involved, the sinner as well as the faithful one. Though forgiveness is possible, and grace abounds, there are still consequences for sin. Even when King

David confessed his transgressions and turned back to God, there were consequences from his sins of adultery and murder. God can be trusted with all aspects of the situation.

Second, it assumes that everything will go well for the sinful spouse in a remarriage. Unless there is a complete transformation, repentance, and surrender to God, the same prideful choices that brought about the unfaithfulness in the first marriage will also be seen in areas of that person's heart in a second marriage. The unfaithfulness is not an isolated event.

A third assumption is that the current marriage will always be hurting, struggling to forgive and fully love again. This is understandable in light of the deep grief now. However, God's grace works in both hearts. It is factual that the impact of unfaithfulness changes a marriage. However, it is also noteworthy that as a marriage seeks the Lord in repentance and surrender, God can heal, rebuild, and bless in amazing ways.

God's love and strength can do a mighty work in both hearts yielded to Him. Every person is a sinner and needs to confess and commit to God's holiness and righteousness. If the unfaithful spouse continues in sin, the faithful spouse can seek the Lord for His will and direction for the future. God still has a plan and promises for the faithful spouse. When we need to know God's will, He will make it clear as we seek Him.

> Ask and it will be given to you; seek and you will find; knock and the door will be opened to you. For everyone who asks receives; he who seeks finds; and to him who knocks, the door will be opened. (Matthew 7:7–8)

Confidence

When a person surrenders painful emotions to the Lord and trusts Him, they can give way to confidence and peace. Our hope is in

Christ, who loves each person immeasurably and guides toward what is right and good. The Lord works in the hearts of both spouses. Each will choose his or her response to the Lord.

Our sovereign God takes bad circumstances and brings good out of them. He convicts and heals hearts. When spouses seek Him, He turns marriages around and plants them on solid ground. Knowing Jesus Christ and surrendering plans and desires to Him is the only way to live by faith and know His will. Real confidence is trusting in God. The Lord will comfort, guide, and bless in amazing ways.

> And we know that in all things God works for the good of those who love him, who have been called according to his purpose. (Romans 8:28)

> The Spirit of the Sovereign LORD is on me,
>   because the LORD has anointed me
>   to preach good news to the poor.
> He has sent me to bind up the broken-hearted,
>   to proclaim freedom for the captives
>   and release from darkness for the prisoners ....
>   (Isaiah 61:1)

The Offending Spouse's Emotions

Shock and Denial

When trust has been broken in a marriage, shock and denial are emotions the offending spouse feels also but usually for different reasons. A spouse who has shattered the trust in marriage is shocked because the sins have been found out and the secret is revealed. What he or she had carefully hidden is now suddenly undeniable.

Anger

The sinful spouse is usually angry because sins were found out. This angry attitude is more concerned about being found out than the impacts of the hurtful actions. Also the anger can be focused on the possible personal consequences. This is a reflection of how the offending spouse has minimized and rationalized the offenses.

Sometimes offending spouses can have a change of heart, feeling angry at themselves when they realize how wrong their actions were. Such a spouse wants to acknowledge the sins done and begin the right steps toward godly sorrow and repentance. This anger is the beginning of heart renewal and recommitment to the marriage.

Relief

The unfaithful spouse may actually feel a sense of relief when the wrong actions are revealed. This relief comes from realizing that the deception can finally end. There is an uncanny emotional relaxing with the realization that there is no longer a need to hide the sins, even though great efforts went into maintaining the deception.

A misleading feeling is that "the worst is over." That is not accurate for either spouse. The offending spouse must come completely clean of the offenses, and the hurting spouse will have increased pain and sadness in the process. Hopefully, when appropriate actions are taken, the marriage gets stronger. There may not be complete relief for quite a while.

Remorse, Sorrow, and Shame

When an offending spouse sees her violation as it actually is and realizes the sinful heart that brought it about, hopefully this will lead to genuine and appropriate remorse. However, the spouse's emotions need to be carefully supervised. An offending spouse may experience so much shame and remorse that he or she becomes suicidal or unstable.

This is serious and requires immediate attention. Someone needs to ask questions regarding any earlier suicide attempts and methods. The current possibilities need to be carefully explored. Collaborate and take steps to minimize the immediate viable options. Ideations can turn to plans if not addressed adequately. Call in help as needed.

Uncertainty and Apprehension

Some offending spouses try to control the partner's negative response by suggesting it first. For example, "If you leave me, I understand." This gives a mixed message, distracts from the best course of action, and focuses on separation instead of restoration. A much better statement would be "I know you could leave me, but I hope you won't. I will work to become trustworthy and to rebuild your confidence in me."

The unfaithful spouse's sense of uncertainty about how the faithful spouse will react is understandable. However, walking on eggshells is not beneficial. The faithful spouse will be more convinced of repentance when the other spouse is proactive and diligent to begin serving, acting in love, carrying the appropriate share of responsibilities and treating the faithful spouse with respect and appreciation.

Emotions versus Decisions

God gives emotions to help people experience and feel what happens in life. Emotions reflect God's creativity in how He made people. Emotions are important for processing relationships and experiences. However, God did not intend that we stay wrapped up in emotions or immobilized in them. He does not want us to let them drive our life. Decisions are to be made with our mind and our will. We choose to take right actions and to obey God even when the emotions may be different. Take caution that emotions don't become the main emphasis. Validate feelings, and move to make commitments and decisions based on biblical truth and faith.

10

Forgiveness

Blessed is he
whose transgressions are forgiven,
whose sins are covered.
Blessed is the man
whose sin the LORD does not count against him
and in whose spirit is no deceit.
—Psalm 32:1–2

Forgiveness is a marvelous, amazing gift from God. God incarnate, Jesus Christ, came to earth. He lived a perfect life, died the most horrific death of crucifixion, and rose from the dead to provide atonement for our sins. The redemption that God provides for us offers forgiveness for our sins. God gives the opportunity for a personal relationship with Jesus Christ when by faith a person accepts His gift of grace (Ephesians 2:8). God's forgiveness is from His love and mercy.

Everyone needs Jesus Christ as Savior. Everyone needs forgiveness. Paul stated that "all have sinned and fall short of the glory of God" (Romans 3:23) and that "the wages of sin is death, but the gift of God is eternal life in Christ Jesus our Lord" (Romans 6:23). Jesus talked about the need to be "born again." He said, "For God so loved the world that he gave his one and only Son, that whoever believes in him shall not perish but have eternal life" (John 3:16). He was talking about Himself as the only Son of God.

Paul explained, "If you declare with your mouth, 'Jesus is Lord,' and believe in your heart that God raised him from the dead, you will be saved. For it is with your heart that you believe and are justified, and it is with your mouth that you confess and are saved" (Romans 10:9–10). When people pray, confessing their sins and asking Jesus Christ to be their Savior, God faithfully saves them.

Christians can have the assurance of salvation. "Yet to all who received Him, to those who believed in his name, he gave the right to become children of God" (John 1:12). In Romans 10:13, Paul stated, "Everyone who calls on the name of the Lord will be saved." John wrote, "I write these things to you who believe in the name of the Son of God so that you may know that you have eternal life" (1 John 5:13).

The Bible teaches that the forgiveness and salvation we so desperately need can only be provided through Jesus Christ. Peter stated, "Salvation is found in no one else, for there is no other name under heaven given to men by which we must be saved" (Acts 4:12). God provides the spiritual payment for sins. God gives us forgiveness unto salvation. He instructs us to let His forgiveness empower us to release the emotional and relational pain caused by sins from others. This is what happens when we forgive others who sin against us.

What Forgiveness Is

The Greek word often translated in the New Testament as "forgive" means to let go or to release from obligation, to cancel the debt. In Matthew 18:23–35, Jesus told a parable of a king who decided to demand payment from a servant who owed him a huge debt. The servant was unable to pay and asked for more time to pay the king back. The king had mercy on the servant, forgave him, canceled the debt, and let him go.

This servant then encountered another servant who owed him a small amount. He was unwilling to forgive him and had him thrown in jail. Some other servants observed what had happened and reported it to the king. The king called the first servant back in and said, "Shouldn't you have had mercy on your fellow servant just as I had on you?"

In anger the king handed him over to the jailers to be tortured till he paid back all he owed. Jesus said "This is how my heavenly Father will treat each of you if you do not forgive your brother or sister from your heart" (Matthew 18:35). The king forgiving the huge debt is symbolic of the forgiveness God gives to us. The servant who owed a small amount is symbolic of others' sins against us.

God forgives us when we confess and ask Him for forgiveness. He instructs us to forgive others. Forgiveness, like trusting God, requires faith in God and is not based on human feelings. Forgiveness is choosing to trust God, who instructed us to forgive. Emotionally a person may not want to forgive others but chooses to forgive to order to honor and obey God. God in His love blesses us as we choose to forgive others.

Forgiveness frees us. Forgiveness can prevent crushing pain from turning into bitterness that can shackle a person's heart. God instructs us to forgive because it helps *us*. God commands that we forgive, because He loves *us*. God knows that bitterness, rage, anger, malice (desire for revenge), resentment, and hatred can destroy us. These emotions harm the person who was sinned against, not the person who committed the sinful action. The longer these emotions are held on to, the more damage they do.

> Get rid of all bitterness, rage and anger, brawling
> and slander, along with every form of malice.
> (Ephesians 4:31)

Forgiveness comes from God when we confess and repent of our sins. Forgiveness also means that we give the pain to God when others sin against us. None of us deserves God's forgiveness. Neither is our need to forgive others based on whether we think that person deserves forgiveness or not. The forgiveness that God gives us is based on His grace. In the same way, when we forgive someone, we extend grace to that person because God has shown grace to us.

Jesus Christ died on the cross to pay the price for sin, offering us forgiveness and eternal life. We forgive others because Jesus Christ has forgiven us. We forgive, because we have been forgiven. God gives us grace and the ability to treat others with grace.

> Be kind and compassionate to one another, forgiving each other, just as in Christ God forgave you. (Ephesians 4:32)

Forgiveness is very hard when the trust in a marriage has been broken. Forgiveness does not minimize or brush aside the sinful behaviors. The fact that forgiveness is needed confirms that a significant, hurtful sin has occurred. Sin is devastating. It knocks the wind out of the marriage and results in overwhelming pain. Sometimes the initial desire is to give up, walk away (or run away), and quit trying.

Sometimes there is a desire to hang on to the anger and pain, making the offending spouse pay and remember the betrayal. It seems impossible to forgive or to even want to. The truth, however, is that allowing our emotions to determine our choices and actions will only bring more sadness and destruction. Forgiveness proclaims God's amazing love, grace, and mercy.

Forgiveness is from God. Forgiveness is counterintuitive from the human heart. Overriding emotions to obey biblical instructions about forgiveness allows God's grace to work in a life-changing way. God gives us forgiveness and commands that we forgive others. This is a gift not just for them but also for us. Our forgiveness to others means giving to the Lord the pain caused by the sins of others. He alone is able to deal with transgressions and heal hearts.

Forgiveness begins with an initial decision and includes a process. It includes intentional prayer, asking for God's help to shift the focus to Him and off painful emotions and circumstances. God provides the remedy for sin through His grace. The solution for sin is always God's grace. It is grace for those who repent from sin and for those who have been harmed by it.

What Forgiveness Is Not

Forgiveness Is Not Condoning Sin

Forgiveness is needed because something wrong happened that was significant, and it hurts deeply. Forgiveness is not glossing over something or looking the other way. God never winks at or minimizes sin. Forgiveness does not take away justice or omit accountability. Forgiveness requires what is right. It increases the movement toward righteousness.

A main characteristic of forgiveness is that it is a gift that God gives to the hurting spouse to surrender the pain caused by the offenses of another. Forgiveness allows one to release to the Lord the devastation and destruction resulting from ravaging sin. God did not create us to be able to bear the pain and heartbreak of sin. God says give it to Him (1 Peter 5:7).

The handoff occurs in prayer. We offload to God the hurt, disappointment, betrayal, anger, grief, confusion, and every other emotion produced in the aftermath of sin. God is the Lord, the only Savior. He died for all transgressions, understands all the sinful brokenness of mankind, cares about every detail of our lives, and loves us with an eternal love.

Forgiveness does not remove the consequences for the offense. The Bible teaches that there are consequences to sin. Sometimes it seems sinful actions do not result in punishment and repercussions.

However, the Bible teaches that there are negative results from sin. Sin is damaging and can bring havoc to a person's life and to others. The Bible says God is trustworthy about judging sins and acting in mercy and grace.

> Nothing in all creation is hidden from God's sight. Everything is uncovered and laid bare before the eyes of him to whom we must give account. (Hebrews 4:13)

Forgiveness Is Not the Same as Reconciliation or Restoration

Forgiveness is not synonymous with reconciliation and restoration. Forgiveness alone does not reinstate a person or make everything okay in a relationship. Yes, a wounded spouse needs to forgive the spouse who broke the trust. The offending spouse needs to rebuild trust. Forgiveness will begin healing the hearts of the hurting spouse and the offending spouse. However, relationship restoration does not happen until there has been confession, new accountability, consistent repentance, and renewed trust.

Forgiveness Is Not Pretending That Sin Never Happened

Sometimes it is said that forgiveness means the offenses will never be brought up again. However, this is not completely true or always possible. Yes, forgiveness means that offenses are not to be used as a hammer against the offender, but there are times the sins need to be addressed, not just ignored or glossed over as if they never happened. This is especially true in the process of full confession and disclosure. These often take time. Also, it is necessary in the stage of rebuilding accountability. The sins need to be discussed as to how they happened and how to avoid the betrayal happening again.

Forgiveness addresses past actions. After processing them, there can be movement forward with new growth and recommitment.

The offender needs to fully and honestly disclose with a willingness to take the time to deal with the offenses in all the necessary ways. It is not the sinner who should say, "Let's move forward." Instead, his or her focus should stay on genuine humility and godly sorrow. The person who is forgiving will be the one who begins to move forward after hearing and seeing evidence of genuine confession and repentance.

Another misconception about forgiveness is that it is synonymous with forgetting. The old cliché "forgive and forget" is superficial and inaccurate. God never requires that we forget. God has created people with amazing memory capability. Forgiving does not mean that we have no recall of the offenses. No one can just turn off what they remember. Forgiveness means that in the midst of difficult memories, there can still be a miraculous healing because of God's love of us. One doesn't have to forget to forgive. We can choose not to focus on remembering the sins that were done against us.

Forgiveness Is Not Easy

Forgiveness is not easy. Forgiveness affects emotions differently depending on which person it involves. An offending spouse who has sinned and confessed to God and to the other spouse may feel a great sense of relief, joy, and gratitude that comes with forgiveness from God. The faithful spouse may be thankful for God's mercy and grace but at the same time wish the offending spouse would have to undergo consequences and lingering punitive measures. We can trust God with whatever consequences are needed.

We may welcome God's forgiveness in our own life but be less appreciative of it in the life of one who hurt us. The biblical story of Jonah is a good example. Jonah was glad that God was a forgiving God for him but angry that God so quickly and completely forgave the people of Nineveh. He knew that God would respond with mercy if they repented (Jonah 4:1–2). That was why he didn't want to preach repentance to them.

One needs to ask God for help in being thankful for the forgiveness for another as well as for oneself. This is especially true when the faithful spouse feels that he or she has been trustworthy, trying to do right, while the other was unfaithful and irresponsible. In story that Jesus told in Luke 15:29–30, the older brother felt this about his younger prodigal brother.

God is amazing to forgive us so we can receive His salvation. God instructs that we should forgive others because we have been forgiven (Matthew 6:14–15). Sometimes when trust has been broken in a marriage, a hurting spouse may desire to stay married but in reality is not willing to forgive. Choosing to stay married but to hold on to bitterness is not a biblical option.

It is not possible to maintain anger and bitterness and at the same time genuinely forgive as we have been commanded to do. People have to make a conscious decision to forgive. It does not just happen. The decision may need to be made over and again. Usually, when the difficult emotions come again, the decision to forgive has to be renewed. Luke 17:4 and Matthew 18:21–22 both show that forgiveness often needs to occur multiple times.

Anger and bitterness must be replaced with kindness, compassion, and forgiveness. This is choosing to act in love. Even when struggling with emotions, committing to forgive is right. This flows from the willing decision to obey and trust God. This is not possible in our own strength. It is only possible with the power of the Holy Spirit, who indwells us who are Christians. God alone supernaturally empowers us to do right when we seek Him. God blesses us when we obey Him.

Emerson and Daphne were up and down emotionally in the aftermath of his unfaithfulness. They both recommitted to the marriage early in the process with an expressed desire to stay married and seek complete restoration. However, periodically painful memories overwhelmed her, and Daphne found herself drowning in the anger again. She didn't want to be with Emerson and didn't want to be without him either.

She thought, *I can stay married and make him pay.* Trying to make a spouse pay for sinful actions can easily get out of control and limit restoration. The more Daphne hung on to the pain and anger, the more she experienced deep personal sorrow and destructive emotional patterns. In desperation, Daphne yielded to God her immense grief. She chose to trust God with the accounting of Emerson's sins. A load was lifted from her heart. Her joy began to return. She realized that God is loving, righteous, and holy.

God hates sin but loves sinners. Jesus Christ died for sins through His ultimate sacrificial death and became the atonement for all who receive Him as Lord and Savior. If God, who is righteous, is willing to forgive sinners, then how can we who are unrighteous deny forgiveness to them? The sins of others against us are much less than our heart of sin against God. God takes away the guilt of sin and our shame and replaces them with hope and new life in Christ (2 Corinthians 5:17–20).

Forgiveness Is Not Just Saying the Word

Genuine forgiveness is choosing to let go of the violation and trespass against us. The only thing that can ever pay for sin is the blood of Jesus Christ. Nothing is sufficient on a human level. That is why forgiveness is a gift from God. We cannot fathom it, but we can receive it by faith. As the Bible says, "Thanks be to God for his indescribable gift!" (2 Corinthians 9:15).

Forgiveness is an important step toward healing and reconciliation. Forgiveness allows a person to participate in something that only God could have designed and established. It is beyond human understanding. It comes from the heart of God and reflects the character of God. Forgiveness enables one to receive and to give a blessing. It is a powerful way to experience God's grace personally and to give it relationally.

Forgiveness requires letting go of the desire for revenge.

Continually thinking about the wrong actions will only increase the rage and sense of injustice. Blinding anger can steal your strength and direction in life. The temptation is to hold on to the sense of disregard and ruminate on the betrayals. This will hurt the person who was sinned against.

Sometimes there is a hesitation to "reinstate" the spouse who broke the marital trust. While Lane was participating in sexual sins with others, Glenda was handling all the family responsibilities, working hard, and caring for their children. Since then Lane has returned to his family sorrowful and repentant. Glenda accepted him back and wants to forgive, but bitterness floods over her. She asks old questions that have no satisfying answers.

Lane is growing in trustworthiness, committing daily to walk in holiness and purity. Glenda is hesitant to allow him to resume his partnership in any way. She wants to maintain her control of decisions, spiritual leadership, finances, and discipline of the children. It is hard for her to surrender responsibilities back to Lane because his actions were selfish and untrustworthy. Lane needs to patiently trust God with his "reentry".

It is important for Glenda to give her pain to God, asking Him to help her know how to move forward in trusting Lane. Shifting leadership back to Lane in appropriate ways will be a big step toward bringing healing to her heart and healthy equilibrium back to the family.

Questions about Forgiveness

Can a person forgive oneself?

An often heard statement is "I just can't forgive myself". Most of the time, this statement means, "I still have sorrow and regrets about my sin." Reading the whole Bible through, it would be difficult to find one verse that instructs us to forgive ourselves. We do not have the power or the authority to forgive our own sins. If we could, we would not need a Savior. The two kinds of forgiveness are (1) from God and (2) for others. When a person has guilt feelings, it is helpful to ask, "Am I feeling appropriate or inappropriate guilt?"

Appropriate guilt results from sin that has not yet been acknowledged and confessed fully to God and to those sinned against. Appropriate guilt comes after sin occurs and before confession. The Holy Spirit convicts of sin and draws a person toward confession. After sins have been confessed to God, the Lord removes the guilt through forgiveness. If a person still feels guilty after confession, the feelings may be a conviction by the Holy Spirit to confess more fully or to actually receive the forgiveness by faith.

Inappropriate guilt can come from guilt feelings that are not based on actual sins or from not feeling forgiven after confession. Perhaps a person assumes responsibility for something that is not his or her sin. This can bring guilt feelings. When a person does not feel forgiven after forgiveness is given, even after complete confession, a person may still feel great sorrow for the sins done. That is understandable and common. Continuing sorrow about sins does not mean one has not been forgiven.

Sorrow for sins committed can serve as a deterrent to future sins. There is often grief about past sins even when a person has the confidence that God has forgiven them. Confidence about forgiveness is based on faith in God and the Bible, not on emotions. Jesus Christ died on the cross to offer the forgiveness for sins. Emotions can be a mixed bag of gratitude and joy, resulting from forgiveness, and the sorrow of remembering past sins.

When sins have been confessed adequately, guilt has been dealt with spiritually. One should accept God's promised forgiveness by faith. Confession and forgiveness do not take away all the sad emotions. To doubt God's forgiveness because of emotions of regret and sorrow is to misunderstand forgiveness. Forgiveness from God deals with the spiritual payment for sins.

> If we confess our sins, he is faithful and just and
> will forgive us our sins and purify us from all
> unrighteousness. (1 John 1:9)

Should I Remind My Spouse That He or She Is Supposed to Forgive Me?

Micah and Jamie were struggling in the aftermath of his affairs. Micah said he was sorry and claimed that he would be repentant. Jamie was devastated and trying to seek the Lord's comfort and guidance. Micah showed her verses almost daily about forgiveness, telling her, "You just need to forgive me." Instead he should have been studying verses about sinful behavior, confession, repentance, and godly sorrow. He should be mindful of his own need for humility and a changed heart.

The Bible addresses sin and the need for forgiveness. Each person should read the Bible personally, seeking to apply it to oneself. The Bible is not to be a hammer to piously use against another person. Confession, repentance, and recommitment to holiness are the responsibilities of one who has sinned. Forgiveness is the responsibility of the one who was sinned against.

An offending spouse may wrongly think, *When my spouse forgives me, we will be restored.* This is presumptuous and may be untrue. Forgiveness can occur soon after confession. However, restoration happens after the offending spouse has rebuilt the trust. Restoration may happen much later than forgiveness.

At different times in life both aspects of offering and receiving forgiveness can involve each person. Sometimes one spouse has sinned in some way and needs to confess and ask for forgiveness. At another time the other spouse may sin and need to confess and ask for forgiveness. We are all capable of sin and also of feeling hurt when sinned against.

Do I Have to Contact the Other Person to Tell Them They Are Forgiven?

Another misconception is that forgiveness requires telling the other person that he or she is forgiven. Forgiveness is required, but informing the offender is not always necessary. For example, if a house is robbed, the homeowner will be terribly sinned against. Forgiveness trusts God to deal with the injustice. It allows the homeowner to release to the Lord the sad feelings of being violated, and it also helps bring emotional healing.

At this stage, forgiveness is between that hurt person and God. I would not simply counsel a person to go back and tell a thief or a rapist they are forgiven unless that offender confesses and asks for forgiveness.

If an offending person is granted forgiveness before confessing and acknowledging sins and asking for forgiveness, that person may wrongly assume that nothing is required of him. That person may be less responsive to the conviction of the Holy Spirit for the necessary steps toward restoration.

After an offending spouse or someone in an ongoing relationship confesses and asks for forgiveness, then it is important to forgive and to communicate to that person that he or she is forgiven. This will be encouraging and hopefully will be a meaningful early step toward restoration. Withholding the affirmation of forgiveness to a person who has confessed and asked for forgiveness is not appropriate. That can be very discouraging and unkind for the one seeking forgiveness and arrogant for the one withholding it.

> Now instead, you ought to forgive and comfort him, so that he will not be overwhelmed by excessive sorrow. (2 Corinthians 2:7)

Confessing, asking for forgiveness, and committing to repentance are all needed for restoration and rebuilding trust. Forgiveness should come early in the process but not cancel out the other very important phases of the restoration and renewal commitments.

How Can I Give My Pain to God?

Forgiveness does not take away all the pain. However, choosing to trust God's love and His righteousness brings confidence and comfort. Forgiveness means that we know that God deals with all aspects of the sin and will also bring healing to the broken heart. God helps us understand and experience even more of what He has done for us. We all need the forgiveness of God. As we forgive others who sin against us, we understand God's grace even more.

Forgiving others means transferring to God the pain of the offenses done against us. It is relinquishing to Him the sadness and negative impact from the sins. If an offended person holds on to the pain, the anguish of sin and betrayal is crushing and overwhelming. Replacing it with the peace of God's love removes a huge weight and lightens the heart's burden.

The command to forgive others is a blessing that God gives to us and to others. We were not created to bear the pain and sorrow caused by the sins of others. It is too devastating and destructive. Neither are we able to direct the consequences for another person's sins. Only our righteous God has the authority and power to do that. Jesus Christ alone can carry the depth of anguish that sin brings. Forgiveness allows one to give it to Him. Forgiveness brings healing to the heart of the offended and the offender. It restores joy in life.

One might ask "How can I give my pain to God?" This is done through prayer, pouring thoughts and feelings out to Him. God is always tenderly attentive to us. He hears every word and the feelings of every heart. God loves us. He fully knows what it feels like to be mistreated and harmed by others, to be rejected and treated harshly and unkindly. He understands being disappointed, lied to, and receiving the blunt of prideful, selfish sin. He empathizes with those who experience disregard and cruelty from others. He knows the suffering of every sin imaginable. He has endured all that pain for us on the cross.

Jesus Christ invites us to give Him every sorrow from everything that anyone does to sin against us. This is a treasure He gives to us. Many times people think that forgiveness is more about what we do for those who sin against us. However, God's design is first that forgiveness be a huge blessing to us. Forgiveness is something that happens in our heart when we choose to be obedient to Jesus Christ. Trusting God to deal with sin as only He can, and trusting Him with our deepest emotions and struggles, is always right. God is completely faithful and loving.

What Are the Benefits and Blessings from Forgiving Others?

Many blessings result from forgiveness. The greatest is that of obedience to God. Other benefits pertain to the positive results in marriages, families, and other relationships. Forgiveness changes hearts and lives for the better. Some results even improve the physical health of individuals. Those who forgive the transgressions of others have been found to have lower blood pressure and fewer depressive symptoms. At middle age, they experience better overall physical and mental health than those who have not forgiven others in life.

The Prepare/Enrich Forgiveness Scale of Life Innovations Inventories measure a couple's perceptions of their ability to forgive one another following conflict, betrayal, or hurt. They measure how they both request and grant forgiveness. In a 2010 study of 7,034 married couples, Larson and Olson of Prepare/Enrich found that over 86 percent of the vitalized couples had forgiveness as a relationship strength. Less than 1 percent of devitalized couples reported a healthy ability to forgive one another, indicating this was a needed growth area in their relationship.[1] Forgiveness is an important aspect in the relationships of happy, healthy couples.

The pain from broken trust in a marriage is one of the deepest hurts anyone can experience. Forgiveness breaks the desire for revenge. It shifts the focus back to all that God has done for us and fills a heart with gratitude. Sometimes spouses ask, "Can I really forgive my spouse? Can our marriage really be different?" The answer is yes. God will help marriages experience forgiveness and will bring healing and restoration. He does amazing things when we trust Him.

Part 3
Restoration

11

Triggers and Temptations

For the LORD gives wisdom,
and from his mouth come knowledge and understanding.
He holds victory in store for the upright,
he is a shield to those whose walk is blameless,
for he guards the course of the just
and protects the way of his faithful ones.

—Proverbs 2:6–8

The progression is rarely a surprise. Temptations and triggers engage human nature's lust for personal desires. Yielding to idolatrous yearnings rapidly seduces a heart toward the tunnel vision of whatever it takes to satisfy them. Sinful actions usually follow that destroy the trust in marriage. The collateral damage is deep and painful, with huge ramifications.

Addressing temptations and triggers provides the help needed to recognize them, the discernment to choose what's right, and the ability to stop destructive patterns. Sinful actions do not just happen suddenly, like a blowout. Instead, they are the culmination of slow leaks from repeated selfish choices that ignore biblical priorities and standards.

We need to understand who God is and His plan for our lives. Godliness chooses holiness and results in a joy-filled life.

Often believers do not know what the tools and resources are that God has given to provide strength and help against temptations. Knowing what the Bible teaches about temptations and how to respond to them in order to live victoriously is very important.

Temptations

Sources and Descriptions of Temptations

The Bible teaches that temptations come from three sources: *the human heart, Satan,* and *the world.* These three coordinate together. The heart lusts after fleshly desires and self-gratification. Satan puts a hook in it and then lures it away. The world gives many possibilities for sin.

> But each one is tempted when, by his own evil desire, he is dragged away and enticed. Then, after desire has conceived, it gives birth to sin; and sin, when it is full-grown, gives birth to death. (James 1:14–15)

Wisdom and discernment are required to live holy and committed lives. It is important to understand how to recognize temptations in order to stand strong against them. Temptations come unexpectedly and insidiously. They can blindside someone when least expected. Satan and the human heart are clever and persistent. The world offers a vast array of captivating options.

> The heart is deceitful above all things
>   and beyond cure.
> Who can understand it? (Jeremiah 17:9)

Temptations appeal to the human nature, the heart, of every person. Human nature is full of personal longings for power, control, self-exaltation, greed, sexual engagement, pleasure, ease, praise, money, and reputation, with many more. This means that circumstances and relationships in life are often viewed through the lens of "How does this impact me?" or "How can I get what I want?"

Pride is the root of all sin. This is not just being proud of accomplishments. It means seeking to satisfy personal cravings. There is also even a desire for God to do exactly what one wants Him to do in life. Personal kingdom mentality is placing oneself on the throne of one's life and wanting the whole world to revolve around self. However, God is Lord, and He alone deserves to be the epicenter of our life. He alone is worthy of worship.

Ask: "What do I want so desperately that I am resolved to get it no matter what? What do I desire so strongly that I will disobey God's principles to have it?" Whatever that is, it is desired too much. Things can appear benign at first and even understandable; then they can quickly change to reveal blatant selfishness.

For example, if a husband, after a hard day at work, calls his wife on the way home and asks her if he could have about ten or fifteen minutes when he gets home to read the paper and unwind. She agrees. When he arrives home, he kisses his wife, hugs his children, and begins to read the paper. His wife tells the children to let Daddy rest for a few minutes. They agree and go off to play.

Shortly, his sweet little children are running through dragging toys and laughing. Dad says, "Okay, kids, remember, Dad needs a little rest. Go play." He calls to the kitchen where his wife is finishing dinner and says, "Hey, I'd like a little time." She comes out and leads the children away. However, they soon forget and come back, climbing onto his chair and asking him to play. He slams the paper down and angrily yells, "What does a guy have to do around here to get a little peace and quiet?"

His personal desire has grown into full-blown selfishness and sinful disregard toward those to whom he should be the most loving. And why? Because his personal kingdom's desire for everyone to do exactly what he wanted was thwarted. At that moment he cared much more about himself than he did about his family, who are some of God's precious gifts to him. Dad wants to be respected, but he justifies his disrespect toward his family.

The solution to sinful selfishness is to die to self and live for Jesus Christ.

> I have been crucified with Christ and I no longer live, but Christ lives in me. The life I now live in the body, I live by faith in the Son of God, who loved me and gave himself for me. (Galatians 2:20)

This is impossible to do in one's own strength, but is possible by faith in God. Being crucified in Christ means surrendering our life to Him daily. Knowing Jesus Christ, growing in love for Him, and realizing all He has done for us creates a growing desire to live in His power and yield to His will.

Recognizing Temptations

Temptations begin in thoughts and often come in two parts. The first part connects with human desires and sounds truthful. The second part is the enticing lie. A few examples may be: (1) "God gave you this sex drive, didn't He? Doesn't He allow you to satisfy it?" (2) "Sure, you made a commitment not to do this. However, this one time won't be a problem." (3) "Yes, you need to be honest with your spouse. But lying about this one small detail won't hurt anything." (4) "Yes, God said He cares for you. But where is He now in these struggles?" We could go on and on.

Many times temptations appear inconsequential. "This is a small, innocent action right now. It only involves me and won't hurt anyone else." This is not true. In reality, the "ripple effect" and even "wave affect," with ongoing ramifications, can encompass many people for a long time. It can bring more harm and pain than ever imagined. When temptations appear small, take a step back.

Be reminded of the following verse and say "No!" as you remember the big perspective.

> For the grace of God that brings salvation has appeared to all men. It teaches us to say "No" to ungodliness and worldly passions, and to live self-controlled, upright and godly lives in this present age, while we wait for the blessed hope—the glorious appearing of our great God and Savior, Jesus Christ. (Titus 2:11–13)

God's grace empowers us to say no to temptations and to live godly lives. This magnificent passage of scripture is the original "Just say no!" Also, this is the panoramic view of God's grace, including past, present, and future. This verse teaches us that the grace of God brought salvation in the past. That same grace gives us the power to say "No!" to ungodliness and worldly passions and instead to live self-controlled, upright, and godly lives in this present age. We will see God's grace in the future as we wait for Christ's glorious return.

Temptations grab emotions like a magnet. They minimize the offense. Realize the selfishness and crushing blows of sin. Think about the lasting destructive effects of transgressions. Look at this verse to see the pull of sin realistically. Get the big picture of the impacts. Say no to temptations. Enticements shrink in power and charm when we remember God's grace and all He has done for us in the past and the present and will do in the future.

Sinful downfalls are a climax of compromised convictions. Giving in to temptations diminishes spiritual discernment. It is a slippery slope to repeatedly ignore warnings or dismiss conviction from the Holy Spirit. Sin is alluring, and lustful desires lead to deliberate justifications and actions. These choices become patterns and grow into rituals of planned and predictable behaviors. They lead to habitual sin and bondage.

When a pattern of sin begins, it includes anticipated steps that build on each other until the desired outcome results. Intentionality and deliberation become integral parts of the process. Hiding and deception require planning and pretense. Whether a husband is conniving to meet an adulterous partner again or a wife is hiding alcohol to pull out later secretly, they both are engaging in rituals that lead to wrong actions.

Responding to Temptations

Temptations need a strong response. When temptations come, each person should prepare for spiritual battle by responding the way a warrior responds to a trumpet call to battle. The metaphor is of a soldier putting on all the parts of the armor provided by God, our king. It needs an immediate, strong, and appropriate spiritual response.

In the following verses, we see the resources with which to fight the devil's darts. On goes the belt of truth around the waist. Snap. Then put on the breastplate of righteousness. Click. Click. Put the gospel of peace on your feet. Clonk. Take up the shield of faith. Swish. Put on the helmet of salvation. Clunk. Take up the sword of the Word of God. Ready. Pray. Be alert, and keep on praying.

Each item of defense has a special purpose and important power. Commit to use the provided armor effectively to combat the devil and his attacks. Knowing about the equipment and believing it will protect is not enough without putting it on. God really is our protector and defender. His truth, righteousness, gospel, and salvation and His Word are powerful to protect and strengthen.

> Finally, be strong in the Lord and in his mighty power. Put on the full armor of God so that you can take your stand against the devil's schemes. For our struggle is not against flesh and blood, but against the rulers, against the authorities,

against the powers of this dark world and against the spiritual forces of evil in the heavenly realms. Therefore put on the full armor of God, so that when the day of evil comes, you may be able to stand your ground, and after you have done everything, to stand. Stand firm then, with the belt of truth buckled around your waist, with the breastplate of righteousness in place, and with your feet fitted with the readiness that comes from the gospel of peace. In addition to all this, take up the shield of faith, with which you can extinguish all the flaming arrows of the evil one. Take the helmet of salvation and the sword of the Spirit, which is the word of God.

And pray in the Spirit on all occasions with all kinds of prayers and requests. With this in mind, be alert and always keep on praying for all the saints. (Ephesians 6:10–18)

Satan and demons do not have any of the Lord's powers, knowledge, attributes, or characteristics and have no power against the Lord. The Lord God Almighty is all knowing (omniscient) and all powerful (omnipotent) and is everywhere at all times (omnipresent). Satan has none of these abilities. God alone is God, and there is no other like Him. He has won the absolute victory over Satan, evil, sin, and death.

The world opposes God and His righteousness. The "world" includes the secular and ungodly belief system in which we live. It offers deceptions and enticements that appear beautiful and inviting at first. The Bible teaches that one cannot love this world and God at the same time. A clear choice must be made. One either loves the world and the things in the world or loves God and wants to live for Him.

> Do not love the world or anything in the world.
> If anyone loves the world, the love of the Father
> is not in him. For everything in the world—the
> cravings of sinful man, the lust of his eyes and
> the boasting of what he has and does—comes
> not from the Father but from the world. (1 John
> 2:15-17)

God helps believers live above the intrigues of the world. God gives understanding of what is empty and temporal compared to what is genuine and of true eternal value. When worldly temptations persist, trusting in God through faith means asking Him to transform our hearts and give us strength to live for Him.

Resources against Temptations

Our loving God gives us what we need for life and godliness. The Bible is filled with promises of God's help and strength. Choosing to trust God is the central strategy for being victorious over temptations. Growing as a Christian through prayer and worship helps one stay focused on God.

God provided His Word, the Bible, with clear instructions for life and righteous living. The Bible warns of dangers. It teaches how to avoid pitfalls and how to be strong against temptations. The Holy Spirit and His Word are gifts from God to help Christians stand strong against temptations.

> His divine power has given us everything we need
> for life and godliness through our knowledge of
> him who called us by his own glory and goodness.
> Through these he has given us his very great and
> precious promises, so that through them you may
> participate in the divine nature and escape the
> corruption in the world caused by evil desires. (2
> Peter 1:3–4)

One of the most important ways to stay strong against temptations is to regularly read the Bible. God's Word gives clarity and guidance for right decisions and actions. The Holy Spirit convicts of right and wrong. This is confirmed in Psalm 119: 9–11:

> How can a young man keep his way pure?
>> By living according to your word.
> I seek you with all my heart;
>> do not let me stray from your commands.
> I have hidden your word in my heart
>> that I might not sin against you.

These verses teach that the Bible helps one stand strong when faced with difficult choices about obeying God and choosing righteousness. We put God's Word in our heart with meditation and memorization so we won't sin against Him. This scripture applies to everyone, not just young men.

Jesus Christ, His marvelous love, His sacrificial death and glorious resurrection, and the abundant life He gives all lead us to humbly and gratefully bow our hearts and lives before Him. Because He died for us, let us live for Him!

> And he died for all, that those who live should no
> longer live for themselves but for him who died for
> them and was raised again. (2 Corinthians 5:15)

God provided the Bible to instruct us about how to live righteously. The Bible warns of dangers. It teaches how to avoid pitfalls and deal with temptations. The Holy Spirit indwells, strengthens, and guides the believer. Christians have the Holy Spirit indwelling them. The Holy Spirit convicts of right and wrong and enables believers to live for God.

Ignoring Warnings

Temptations pull someone toward engaging in sinful behavior and avoiding good and right behavior. Doing wrong and not doing right are both sin. As temptations give way to wrong choices, awareness fades about the devastation they bring. Living a holy life for the Lord becomes less of a priority. It is quickly replaced with longings for personal indulgences. Yielding to the tug of war between personal desires and honoring God will stifle spiritual growth.

> Anyone, then, who knows the good he ought to
> do and doesn't do it, sins. (James 4:17)

Imagine a young family going to have a special time at a nearby lake in early spring. The water is cold, so the parents tell the sons not to get in the water. The boys want to obey but feel disappointment. The little guys so hoped to swim. Walking on the edge of the dock with arms outstretched for balance, suddenly, "Oops!" they fall off the dock into the water. In the same way, too often people walk on the edge of the dock of life, trying to get as close as possible without falling in.

Get off the dock and move to solid ground to avoid sin. Stop and think about right values and convictions and the people you should love and be committed to. Think of how your sins would affect them. Temptations ignore and block thoughts about others, ferociously focusing on self. In spiritual struggles, the choice is whether to love God and others or self.

> We demolish arguments and every pretension that
> sets itself up against the knowledge of God, and we
> take captive every thought to make it obedient to
> Christ. (2 Corinthians 10:5)

In 2 Corinthians 10:5, we are taught how to respond to temptations. The military metaphor using the descriptions of waging war, weapons, and taking captives shows the need for strong action. Control destructive mental arguments, not allowing them to lead you astray. Take captive the thoughts, and make them obedient to Christ. Willful decisions override emotions. Turn to God in prayer and obedience.

Learn from bad decisions in the past when you relaxed caution and acted on temptations. Forego fantasizing about sin. Run from compromising situations. Be alert to selfish desires and feelings of entitlement that replace genuine love and integrity. Counterfeits flirt with the offer of alluring pleasures. The longer you contemplate them playfully in your thoughts, the more likely you will fall. Be self-controlled and alert to red flags and alarm bells in your head.

Temptations rarely warn before they appear. They more typically blindside or creep up craftily. As soon as awareness comes, be strong. Remember, little decisions lead to big actions and destructive consequences. Sin can be most persuasive at the beginning stage. Be mindful of ideas and veiled compromises that have a dark side. Pay attention to barricades that are designed to protect. The Holy Spirit convicts all along the way.

Imagine a road leading to a great ravine. Along the way are roadblocks and signs to warn everyone. "The bridge is out! The bridge is out! Don't come this way!" It would be foolish to continue down the road, disregarding the flashing lights and red flags. Yet, often people ignore warnings from the Holy Spirit. Instead they continue, oblivious to the grave danger ahead. Then, driving off the cliff, they realize the consequences and harm that comes from a dismissive attitude.

> The prudent see danger and take refuge,
> but the simple keep going and suffer for it.
> (Proverbs 27:12)

Dealing with Temptations

Temptations are doorways to disappointing and harmful behaviors. Learning to respond with biblical commitments enables a person to say no and stand strong. Turning to God in the face of temptations is the most important step. A person turns to God through prayer. Prayer is shifting the focus from desires and circumstances to the Lord. The Lord gives wisdom and help when one seeks Him. Believers never face temptations alone.

One powerful verse to help overcome temptations makes four promises. The verse, 1 Corinthians 10:13, has specific promises to give strength from the Lord. The four promises: (1) Temptations are common to people. (2) God is faithful. (3) With every temptation, we can say no. (4) When we are tempted, there is a way out.

The most powerful promise is that God is faithful. That amazing truth is the anchor against the storms of temptations. Read the verse, and see the simple and life-changing promises. Memorizing this verse keeps it handy and close when you need it.

> No temptation has seized you except what is common to man. And God is faithful; he will not let you be tempted beyond what you can bear. But when you are tempted, he will also provide a way out so that you can stand up under it. (1 Corinthians 10:13)

Sexual sin is especially destructive to marriage. It brings unique pain and heartbreak. Rebuilding trust after sexual sin has occurred in marriage has difficult challenges. Running from temptations and sin is the first line of defense.

The longer a person entertains temptations, the harder it is to say no. The longer one ponders sinful "solicitations," the less likely it is one will escape without giving in. For example, to avoid sexual sin, it's critical that one not view inappropriate things, participate in masturbation, or engage in inappropriate sexual conversations. These steps lead to areas of struggle and downfall.

> Flee from sexual immorality. All other sins a man commits are outside his body, but he who sins sexually sins against his own body. Do you not know that your body is a temple of the Holy Spirit, who is in you, whom you have received from God? You are not your own; you were bought with a price. Therefore, honor God with your body. (1 Corinthians 6:18–20)

> Submit yourselves, then, to God. Resist the devil, and he will flee from you. (James 4:7)

The Bible instructs us to submit to God's authority. Resist Satan's lies and temptations, and he will flee. The metaphor is like a young child running to his parents when frightened. His parents scoop him up, comforting and protecting him. That's how God responds to us when we go to Him. When tempted, run to God. He will strengthen you to avoid sin and stand strong against temptations.

Triggers

Triggers are people, places, things, or events that spark a reminder from previous wrong behaviors. They create vulnerability toward repeated indiscretions. Knowing and avoiding triggers are pivotal aspects of being tenacious against destructive inclinations. Turning from sins requires clear decisions before the temptation comes.

Avoiding bad familiar places, old friends, or previous activities will be imperative for new commitments. Triggers can bring instant reminders of past interests. If these interests led to past compromises, they can quickly ignite them again.

Staying clear of triggers may mean ending friendships with some people. Even old and lengthy friendships may need to be terminated. Dropping out of certain activities and ending participation in certain organizations or groups may be necessary. Changing driving patterns and familiar routes may be required. Do whatever is needed to avoid previous compromises and distractions.

Complacency and Denial

God's Word gives provisions to stand strong against temptations, including the Bible and His Holy Spirit. Confidence should be in the provisions God has given to deal with temptations, not in personal strength. The following verse teaches that overconfidence in oneself and complacency about temptations brings vulnerability:

> So, if you think you are standing firm, be careful
> that you don't fall! (1 Corinthians 10:12)

It's dangerous when a person is prideful and overconfident or naive and unconcerned about the potential destruction of sin. When one looks away or minimizes temptations, then danger may be just ahead. Wrong choices happen easily. Spiritual apathy is dangerous. Pride denies the sin possibilities. Nonchalance is no plan for spiritual protection. Being smug and overconfident is irresponsible.

Niagara Falls is an example of something of great potential harm if dangers are not recognized. Niagara Falls is a huge area of immense natural waterfalls on the United States–Canadian border. Its massive horseshoe-shaped cataract results from many rivers flowing together. On these rivers, far away from the falls, is where the danger begins. Though the deep rivers seem restful and serene, underneath a tremendous current is gathering, unbeknownst to those in boats on the surface.

From miles back, signs can be seen along the riverbanks

warning boaters of grave dangers ahead. Signs like "Danger Ahead!" "Turn Back!" "Strong Currents!" "No Boats Past This Point" appear along the rivers' edges. The conscientious boater will turn back to safer areas.

However, those who are not paying attention and continue to drift along can suddenly be in a very threatening situation and have great difficulty trying to change course. If they are not able to act quickly enough, they will be swept along without hope or means of rescue.

In the same way, a person can drift along unaware of dangers and pitfalls in life. Being oblivious to the fascinations and inherent concerns can make a person feel a false safety. There is a need to be alert to improprieties and subtle questionable activities and relationships. When triggers and temptations beguilingly lure a person along, immediate attention with changes is needed.

Some Common Triggers

Some common triggers are anger; certain people, events, and places; emotional difficulties; financial strains; struggles; fears; discouragement; victim mentality; laziness; and boredom. Any one of these can cause one to be especially vulnerable and easily led astray. Be aware of rationalizations and small decisions that trigger lusts, personal desires, pleasures, and quick fixes. They begin slyly and seductively and can quickly develop into definite plans. Especially avoid certain people and places that pull toward wrong influences and actions.

Triggers shift to temptations, moving from thoughts to engage emotions and actions. Recognize the signs. Do not minimize the destructive charms. Distance yourself from bad influences and self-consuming thoughts. Pray. Turn to the Lord for the strength you need. Focus your thoughts on God and what honors Him. Think of those you should love and protect. Commit to do what is in their best interest. Reach out to someone who will encourage you to do right. Choose to be holy and loving. Read the Bible. Remember, God helps us say "No!" to wrong desires. Look for the way out, and take it.

Bad Friendships

One of the most common triggers is a bad friendship. Many times friends are instrumental in leading people toward harmful temptations and actions. Friendships may begin when a person is younger and continue for years, even though they are not positive. Sometimes these friendships continue because of a perceived loyalty. Negative friendships need to end. This is imperative even at the risk of hurting another's feelings or receiving disapproval.

Ronald and Leslie argue about his friendships with his old high school buddies. Ronald has become a Christian since he graduated. Most of his old friends are not Christians, but he still gets together with them periodically. Rather than sharing Christ with them, Ronald repeats immature behaviors. Leslie doesn't trust them and doesn't like how Ronald acts when he is around them. She wishes he would end the friendships.

> Do not be yoked together with unbelievers. For what do righteousness and wickedness have in common? Or what fellowship can light have with darkness? (2 Corinthians 6:14)

> Do not be misled: "Bad company corrupts good character." (1 Corinthians 15:33)

We should desire the approval of the Lord, not the approval of people. Our lives should be committed to pleasing God and honoring Him, not trying to please people. The Bible also says that if we try to please people, then we cannot please God. The focus should be on obedience to God and not concern about what other people think.

> Am I now trying to win the approval of men, or of God? Or am I trying to please men? If I were still trying to please men, I would not be a servant of Christ. (Galatians 1:10)

Alcohol

Alcohol is a major trigger in our world today. Alcohol use and abuse touches many aspects of life and relationships. Alcohol is a precipitating factor in countless vehicle accidents as well as domestic abuse, sexual sin, unfaithfulness, and irresponsibility. As a counselor, I am regularly trying to pick up the pieces of lives broken by alcohol.

> Wine is a mocker and beer a brawler;
> whoever is led astray by them is not wise.
> (Proverbs 20:1)

Alarming statistics reveal the negative impacts of alcohol in deaths, automobile crashes, broken families, broken hearts, and out-of-control lives. Although it is not advertised, America is quickly becoming an alcoholic nation. Alcohol is the legal drug in our culture that most negatively affects the largest number of people. It is indescribably destructive to individuals, marriages, and families.

Thomas asked Sally to give up alcohol and her bad behaviors. Sally minimized the negative influence of alcohol. She thought she could continue drinking and keep the right priorities she professed. Loving alcohol more than her marriage, she lost perspective of her commitments and living righteously. Sally lost her moral compass and her marriage.

Social Media

Other common triggers that trip couples up and cause broken trust are the social media. Social media depict a fantasy and a shallow world. Seductive and destructive relationships and habits can begin with contacts and ideas from social media. Often social media get too much attention and rob precious couple and family time. They also feed a craving for what everyone else has and a disregard for the genuine treasures that are actually within reach.

Many safeguards and commitments need to be set up to protect marriages and families from the dangers lurking on the Internet. After someone has broken relationship trust because of involvement on computers and digital devices, that person needs to disconnect from social media completely.

God gives us strength against triggers and temptations. He will give help to everyone who seeks Him. God's guidelines and commandments reveal His protective care for us. He loves everyone with an immense and perfect love. God alone is worthy of our worship. He provides the help to fight temptations and avoid triggers and to stand strong against what is wrong and destructive.

12

Accountability

Let love and faithfulness never leave you;
bind them around your neck,
write them on the tablet of your heart.
Then you will win favor and a good name
in the sight of God and man.
—Proverbs 3:3–4

Importance of Accountability

Accountability is foundational to a strong and healthy marriage. Accountability proves trustworthiness. The Bible teaches that love and faithfulness are vital characteristics of godliness. Proverbs says that wisdom is needed for a person to walk in godliness.

After broken trust in marriage, there must be confession and repentance. Then accountability is needed to establish perimeters in the marriage. Being accountable and adhering to proper disciplines show repentance in action. These are foundational blocks for recommitment, restoration, and renewed joy in marriage.

Accountability is guarding the marriage with faithfulness and commitment. It brings predictability and confidence to relationships. It verifies a heart desiring to be trustworthy and responsible with integrity. Accountability is purposeful and intentional. Genuine accountability is represented by a pledge to openness, transparency, and an eagerness to have things carefully scrutinized.

> Produce fruit in keeping with repentance. (Luke 3:8)

As a night security guard routinely walks around a designated site, he is checking doors, locks, and all patrolled areas. The guard does not want to find anything open or unusual during the checking process. Similarly, accountability proves that everything is protected. Asking for accountability is not "playing gotcha." Instead, it is taking steps to find things are amply secure.

The Right Attitude of Accountability

After the prophet Nathan confronted King David about his adultery with Bathsheba, David offered a humble prayer of acknowledgement and repentance, asking God for forgiveness and cleansing. His prayer is recorded in Psalm 51, and in verse 12, he asked God to grant him the right attitude: "Restore to me the joy of your salvation and grant me a willing spirit, to sustain me."

The attitude needed in rebuilding trust is a willing spirit. David confessed that he could not create the right attitude in his own strength but needed God to give it to him. Believers realize that we do not achieve righteousness by ourselves. Christ's Spirit in us helps us desire it and strengthens us to do it. In order to restore trust through accountability, a willing spirit is essential. In fact, it will sustain or uphold a spouse to persevere through the journey of rebuilding trust through accountability.

> For it is God who works in you to will and to act in
> order to fulfill his good purpose. (Philippians 2:13)

Hesitancy in the face of required accountability may cause one to suspect deception. Protesting and reluctance are huge red flags.

When trust has been broken in marriage, the unfaithful spouse may say he or she wants to be accountable but exhibit a resistant attitude against standards and methods that are requested. This stubbornness reveals the lack of a willing spirit.

> But the things that come out of a person's mouth come from the heart, and these defile them. (Matthew 15:18)

For example, when a person goes through security at the airport, an uncooperative or resistant attitude raises questions and is a sure invitation to be pulled out of the line for closer inspection. When the police stop to question someone, the best response is to be respectful, open, and honest. Defiance and a lack of cooperation cause suspicions.

One may feel that increased accountability is an intrusion on his or her privacy. Instead of resenting this scrutiny, the right attitude is to welcome the opportunity to develop credibility. The unfaithful spouse may try to shift the focus onto other good aspects of his behavior. This is an incorrect approach because even many good actions may not cancel out broken trust.

The faithful spouse cannot play the role of the Holy Spirit, who convicts us of our sin. Being the accountability inspector in a marriage is emotionally exhausting. When the spouse who has been hurt has to do most of the hard work to establish new accountability, it is best to step back and pray. The unfaithful spouse is being spiritually and relationally lazy.

An earnest desire for a spouse to be righteous does not make it happen. Each spouse chooses to be sincerely righteous or not. Seek to honor God with your own life, and pray for your spouse that God will give him or her a willing spirit to become more accountable and a desire to rebuild trust. As your spouse seeks to honor God, he or she will begin to take initiative and assume personal responsibility. That will result in following through with right actions. Until then, no coercing or pleading can bring about a heart change in your spouse.

> The highway of the upright avoids evil;
> he who guards his way guards his life.
> (Proverbs 16:17)

A deliberate and determined effort to avoid evil is compelling evidence that a person sincerely wants to walk in righteousness. An aversion to wrong behaviors motivates a person to adopt strong protective measures against detrimental actions. The person who wants to diligently guard his life is self-motivated and eager to comprehensively put safeguards in place. He does not rely on someone else to convince or to persuade him. This results in discernment and discretion.

The faithful spouse must also have a willing spirit. It is right and gracious to give the other spouse an opportunity to rebuild trust through accountability. An offended spouse may feel that the other spouse does not deserve another chance and that the offending spouse's repentance is not genuine. Unless there is real heart change and surrender to the Lord by the untrustworthy spouse, then all efforts will be superficial. However, when a person is truly repentant and yielded to the lordship of Christ, their heart and actions can change dramatically. Only repentance and accountability over time will reveal the truth.

Characteristics of Accountability

Accountability means *accessibility*. When two people marry, they enter into oneness. Secrecy is left at the door and should not be a part of the marriage. Because of what oneness means biblically, secrecy and privacy are oxymoronic to marriage. Everything in marriage should be unreservedly open and accessible to each spouse. Nothing should be hidden. Accountability is a protection for marriage.

Celeste and Arnold had several discussions about transparency in their marriage. Then Arnold got a new job and began to have personal conversations and lunches with a female coworker. He changed passwords on his phone and computer. Celeste suspected unfaithfulness. Finally, he acknowledged it. Celeste talked with a counselor who could encourage Arnold to disclose what he was hiding and return to his marital commitments.

When temptations get a foothold, sin and secrecy quickly follow. With honesty there is no need to hide anything. Changes in patterns of openness and accountability should not just be overlooked or explained away. Dig deeper. Do not accept flimsy excuses or pretend that nothing is wrong.

Accountability should be *verifiable*. In this culture of technology, cameras, and GPS devices, activities and whereabouts can be verified easily. Phillip wanted to rebuild the trust with Susie. He took pictures with his phone wherever he went to visibly confirm his statements. He was also proactive to disclose all receipts and financial transactions. Susie realized he was sincere about wanting to restore her confidence.

> Whoever walks in integrity walks securely,
>> but whoever takes crooked paths will be
> found out. (Proverbs 10:9)

Accountability includes an *eager attitude* to be forthright. The unfaithful spouse should appreciate the opportunity to rebuild trust. A complete willingness is noticeable and adds to credibility. When a faithful spouse has to try to persuade a spouse to be accountable, the unfaithful spouse clearly does not have the appropriate desire or commitment.

Attitude is as important as actions in accountability. An offending spouse may have a resentful or begrudging attitude, complaining, "This is too hard! "It's unreasonable," "It's impossible to do this," or "It's unfair." Such reactions reveal the spouse is disinclined to do important things to be humble, yielded, and invested to prove sincerity and commitment and to rebuild trust. These indicate a resistant and obstinate heart.

These warning signs cause relationship alarm. These wrong attitudes reveal prideful arrogance and a focus on self as the victim. The hurting spouse is the true victim. The unfaithful spouse is unwilling to do the necessary things. Lack of humility and investment reveal efforts to sabotage needed changes. A faithful spouse may give up hope and doubt there will be true repentance.

Tim had harmed the trust in his marriage. Marsha felt as if they were barely hanging on. Tim became sincerely repentant and accountable with commitment and fervor. His motivation and genuineness were evident in all he did. Her heart took notice. He won back her trust, and their marriage was wonderfully restored.

In contrast, reticence, whining, and complaining reveal a selfish, stubborn heart. Anthony had been unfaithful. He thought he should be able to dictate what was necessary for accountability. He accused Cynthia of holding on to the pain too long. He said she was unreasonable and mean. Actually, she was gracious and patient in what she and the counselor requested of Anthony. His unwillingness to repent of his unfaithfulness resulted in divorce.

Areas for Accountability

Spiritual

In a marriage that has experienced difficulty or unfaithfulness, the greatest goal is not to save the marriage. Rather, it is that both spouses are drawn closer to God, becoming more obedient to Him and committed to spiritual growth. Spiritual accountability is foundational to stronger, renewed marriages and lasting positive changes.

Spiritual actions reveal love for God and righteousness. These are lived out practically in life through commitments to worship services, Bible study, prayer, and acts of loving service toward others. It is appropriate to expect these signs from someone who sincerely wants to grow in the Lord.

Asking someone to commit to spiritual disciplines will bless wonderfully in many ways. Surrendering to the Lord and experiencing His goodness and grace will fill a life with joy. There needs to be clear discussion about how to implement these activities. They can be done together as a couple and individually. A spouse increasing worship, Bible reading, and other Christian activities can share and report what is being learned and applied in life.

Involving an encouraging Christian mentor to walk beside a spouse can be very effective to help that spouse grow and change. Biblical instruction and guidance can bring greater understanding and application. The mentor should always be the same gender as the spouse being helped. This person should talk with the couple together to update them on how things are going. The mentor should be a godly person with integrity and a mature personal walk with the Lord.

> As iron sharpens iron,
> so one person sharpens another. (Proverbs 27:17)

Social Media

> I made a covenant with my eyes
> not to look lustfully at a young woman. (Job 31:1)

> Do not love the world or anything in the world. If anyone loves the world, the love of the Father is not in them. For everything in the world—the cravings of sinful man, the lust of his eyes, and the boasting of what he has and does—comes not from the Father but from the world. (1 John 2:15–16)

Social media is a major area of potential danger to marriages. Great amounts of wisdom and discretion are required in order to protect a marriage from temptations and sin. Many married couples experience unfaithfulness involving social media even though they would never have imagined it could happen to them. Proactive safeguards cannot be overrated. Marriages need protection.

Naivety is no excuse. Prevention is easier than the pain that results from ignoring the dangers. Complete openness with all passwords and social media accounts is crucial. No secret communication with anyone outside the marriage is acceptable. All computers, telephones, tablets, and every other technology device should be available to both spouses at all times with willingness for them to be inspected at any time.

If a spouse has compromised convictions or participated in social media in wrong ways, then that person needs to get off all social media. Social media is not a necessity. Ending all connection with social media needs to be clean and complete. Filters and protections in place on every computer are also recommended for all family members.

Gina had an affair with a high school boyfriend after they connected on Facebook. Her husband, Randy, learned that Gina had been talking with a number of men for the past couple of years. Randy had hoped she was finally going to be trustworthy again. However, she had been reluctant to set up all the safeguards and restrictions that Randy had requested. Instead of rebuilding trust, Gina's lack of accountability was creating greater suspicions.

Communications

All methods of communication with anyone should be open to both spouses. The only exceptions are with professional jobs that require confidential information. Phone passwords, e-mails, texts, and voice messages should be available for spouses to know about at any time. All Internet use should be available for examination at any time. A spouse should not hide his or her phone or any of its information from a spouse.

Communications and conversations should be shared between spouses. Individuals outside the marriage should not know more about a spouse than the married partner knows. Information about contacts should be discussed daily.

Some have asked, "What about old high school friends or family members?" The same safeguards are appropriate. Nothing should be kept secret from the other spouse. Even familiar relationships need guidelines and transparency.

Mitch and Tina disagree about open access to all areas of communication in their marriage. Mitch will commit and then not follow through on what he previously agreed to. He argues about the need for openness, acts as if it's a great burden, changes access codes, and stubbornly justifies his secrecy. Every step back breaks the trust again and breaks Tina's heart. All these red flags should signal for Tina Mitch's lack of integrity.

Time and Schedule

In marriage, couples need to regularly discuss calendars, activities, and whereabouts. Frequently updating schedules and events is important so that spouses can stay informed about each other. Information should be verifiable and transparent. There is no reason why all this information would not be open and available to each other. Hesitation and reluctance may indicate that something is being deliberately hidden.

When a spouse wants to rebuild trust, it is important to establish significant ways to validate activities. Equally, there needs to be a willingness to establish accountability. Spouses should make each other a priority in their schedules and activities. A spouse's requests and questions should be given a lot of attention. Caring about these can show commitment and love.

Gordon shrugs off Leslie's requests to compare calendars and plan for intentional activities together. He says his work schedule is demanding and all-consuming. He doesn't plan ahead for anything with her. However, at other times he's able to make plans to attend sporting events with buddies several weeks ahead. She gets the leftovers of his schedule and wonders how she ranks as a priority to him.

Finances

Rebuilding marital trust regarding finances takes commitment and consistency. The discipline of methodically combing through receipts and recording expenses is a first step. Humbly desiring to regain trust will require complete openness. The goal of renewed believability and a restored marriage is worth every detail and needed action. New disciplines have to be carefully forged even amid desires for selfish freedom and unshackled spending.

Writing things down, keeping records, and being transparent for much longer than might seem necessary are all a part of financial trust building. It isn't just for a limited time, but it is changing entrenched patterns of how money is viewed and used. What's needed is a shift from reckless disorganization and selfish whims to disciplined decisions and predetermined agreements. Partners must choose to permanently recommit to necessary steps of diligence, honesty, and responsible financial actions.

It's essential to discuss income, expenses, upcoming needs, and anticipated bills every week. Welcoming the budgeting process and effort and taking initiative to stay on track are good indicators of sincere effort and commitment. Working as a team instead of complaining about the requirements reveals an open heart to accountability. The formerly untrustworthy spouse needs to be responsible, dependable, and consistent. Appreciate the other spouse who has to deal with past junk and is still willing to give another chance. That is love and grace.

Not again, Michael says to himself as he looks over the credit card monthly statement. *But Julie promised!* His heart sinks more as he looks down the list of purchases. Michael remembers Julie's outings with girlfriends and her shopaholic sister. Whenever he has confronted her about expenses or the need to live on the budget, she angrily responds with "I spend money to make me feel good about myself. Don't you want me to look great and feel like I'm special?" He clearly sees the idolatry of her heart. She is concerned only about herself.

Relationships

> Do not be misled: "Bad company corrupts good character." (1 Corinthians 15:33)

We are influenced by friendships and relationships we build. The Bible warns of relationships that steer us away from the right path. Wisdom and discernment are necessary in order to know the character of people. The Bible says that a person's words and actions reveal character. We can learn much about a person's integrity and values by watching and listening to his or her life. It is also important to realize that often characteristics are visible but overlooked or minimized.

When trust has been broken because of a wrong relationship, priorities need to be reassessed. Changes need to be made that honor the spouse above every other person. Perhaps the marriage has been harmed by adultery, an ungodly friend, or an unseemly business partner. It requires a willing response to honor the spouse and be willing to end destructive friendships.

> The righteous choose their friends carefully,
>> but the way of the wicked leads them astray.
>> (Proverbs 12:26)

Trenton and Teri argue because he does not like her club friends. They spend a lot of money and talk condescendingly about their husbands. He wonders if Teri is disrespectful about him too. Trenton should be the priority relationship in Teri's life. There is a need for a genuine willingness to disconnect from friends who do not have right convictions and commitments.

Sexual Purity

> I will set before my eyes
>> no vile thing.
> The deeds of faithless men I hate;
>> they will not cling to me. (Psalm 101:3)

When a spouse is either caught or confesses involvement with pornography, specific steps are required to rebuild trust in the marriage. Pornography is extremely disrespectful and destructive to the spouse. It devalues marriage and dishonors God. Pornography is progressive. High levels of transparency are required to break the shackles of pornographic bondage. Consistent stringent accountability and necessary counseling serve as catalysts toward rebuilding the trust.

The unfaithful spouse must confess every wrong action. Strong computer filters are important too. There is software that sends e-mails to participants revealing Internet sites accessed as well as frequency and duration. These e-mails are sent to spouses, accountability partners, or whoever else has agreed to be in the accountability loop. Passwords are established and only available to the faithful spouse. This limits using the computer to time together.

Others who walk alongside are helpful. The motivation for purity and accountability needs to be as strong from the spouse who has been involved in pornography as from the faithful spouse. When a spouse who struggles with pornography travels, accountability commitments should include pervasive measures to provide peace of mind for the spouse at home. Some husbands unplug the TV or ask it to be removed from the hotel room.

It is encouraging for a spouse to witness the marriage partner regularly reading the Bible, spending time in prayer, and engaged in worship and in relationship with strong godly encouragers. However, that spouse also needs to also be diligent and fully transparent, accountable, and disciplined, exhibiting a humble attitude with God-honoring actions.

Connie has been hurt many times in her marriage because of Jeff's involvement in pornography. Time and again he promises to change his behaviors and stop sinning. Those commitments are short-lived and easily cast aside for his insatiable appetite for porn. Connie longs for him to understand how it makes her feel filthy and tossed aside. Jeff must take initiative to seek biblical help from a pastor or counselor.

Accountability is deeper and more significant than just changed behavior. It means understanding the biblical view of sexual activity, living right values, and putting aside deception and secrecy. The person who wants to rebuild trust must proactively disconnect from all sources of pornography and reconnect in love and kindness to the spouse. Accountability is about confession, repentance, and holiness.

> Therefore, prepare your minds for action; be self-controlled; set your hope fully on the grace to be given you when Jesus Christ is revealed. As obedient children, do not conform to the evil desires you had when you lived in ignorance. But just as he who called you is holy, so be holy in all you do; for it is written: "Be holy, because I am holy." (1 Peter 1:13–16)

God's Word gives clear help about how to turn from temptation and rely on God's strength to make the right choices. Commit to live for the Lord with your body. Do not be conformed to the world's way of thinking, but renew your mind in Christ. Turn to God for strength and help.

> Therefore, I urge you, brothers, in view of God's mercy, to offer your bodies as living sacrifices, holy and pleasing to God—this is your spiritual act of worship. Do not conform any longer to the pattern of this world, but be transformed by the renewing of your mind. Then you will be able to test and approve what God's will is—his good, pleasing and perfect will. (Romans 12:1–2)

Results of Accountability

Trust is essential in marriage. Accountability is one of the most important focal points of strengthening and restoring trust. When a marriage partner has broken the trust in the marriage, renewed accountability is crucial. Significant steps need to be taken. If there is genuine repentance, willingness for complete transparency, and strong accountability, then there can be healing for the marriage.

Sincere repentance will incorporate new and effective patterns of accountability. These actions of love can fill a heart and a marriage with hope and new direction. This attitude honors God and the spouse. The Lord requires it, the spouse deserves it, and the marriage needs it. A dedication to seek right attitudes and actions can bring changes and a plan for growth. The outcome results are long awaited blessings.

13

Protecting Your Marriage

Above all else, guard your heart,
for it is the wellspring of life.
—Proverbs 4:23

Why It Is Important to Protect Marriage

And this is my prayer: that your love may abound more and more in knowledge and depth of insight, so that you may be able to discern what is best and may be pure and blameless until the day of Christ, filled with the fruit of righteousness that comes through Jesus Christ—to the glory and praise of God. (Philippians 1:9-12)

In life we are faced with many decisions. Some of them are for good instead of bad or best instead of good. This verse teaches that when our love abounds, God's grace gives us discernment to make the best decisions. Some of the most important decisions regarding marriage are about protecting it. Best choices produce lives filled with fruits of righteousness for the glory of God. Protecting marriage wisely has much to do with living for the glory of God.

On September 11, 2001, America was attacked. Prior to that,

the United States did not really know who the enemy was. However, after the attacks on that day, much more was learned about the adversary. Shortly after that a Homeland Security Department was established in the government to protect the country's homeland. Marriages also need homeland security to protect them from the enemy. The Bible teaches to be wise and alert about the adversary.

> Be self-controlled and alert. Your enemy the devil prowls around like a roaring lion looking for someone to devour. (1 Peter 5:8)

My husband and I lead marriage conferences. One of the sessions is on protecting marriage. We find that most couples have not discussed how to safeguard their marriage. Couples need to make commitments about relating to people of the opposite gender outside the marriage. They need to establish guidelines that provide security for each spouse and the marriage.

Usually, spouses assume that they are on the same page about appropriate boundaries in their marriage. However, often they have not discussed these carefully enough. Then when they least expect it, the marital trust may be shattered because of affairs or indiscretions. Married couples need to take time to thoroughly talk through these areas and make commitments to prevent problems before they arise. The enemy, the devil, is certainly beguiling and insidious. The world does not encourage Christ-honoring marriages.

Protecting marriage is better and easier than trying to correct problems after they have occurred. Understanding the dangers of an unprotected marriage is the first step. To treat potential marital hazards as insignificant is to ignore the perils of this world. Wisdom requires that weaknesses are evaluated and guardrails set up to block temptations and protect from calamity. Being aware of enticements protects against attitudes and actions that can threaten marriages.

When discussing marriage protection, it is vital to understand foundational biblical truths. Marriage is a wonderful gift from God. We do not own it. We are the managers of what God has ordained. Husbands and wives are to be good stewards of this marvelous blessing. God intends that we treat marriage as a precious treasure, vigilant to preserve the sacred relationship of a husband and wife.

My husband and I are committed to protecting our marriage for a lifetime and to finish well. We establish safeguards, address issues, and check often to maintain godliness. We want to live our whole life honoring Jesus Christ and each other, not wanting in any way to harm the name of either one. We are both working in ministry and keep our protection commitments strong. The blessings are enduring trust, deep confidence, and joy in marriage.

Areas of Needed Protection

Heart and Mind

The most important area of needed protection in marriage is a heart toward God and toward each other. A heart that seeks the Lord is mindful that we belong to Him and so does our marriage. This heart attitude is one of diligence and obedience. A Christ-honoring heart reveals deep respect in one's actions, attitudes, and relationships.

> One of the teachers of the law came and heard them debating. Noticing that Jesus had given them a good answer, he asked him, "Of all the commandments, which is the most important?"
>
> "The most important one," answered Jesus, "is this: 'Hear, O Israel, the Lord our God, the Lord is one. Love the Lord your God with all your heart and with all your soul and with all your mind and with

all your strength.' The second is this: 'Love your neighbor as yourself.' There is no commandment greater than these." (Mark 12:28–31)

Love God with all your heart, soul, mind, and strength. Then love others with a sacrificial love. Sounds simple and easy. It is simple, but not easy. The human heart tends to get in the way. That is why we need to make sure our hearts and minds are focused on God first and then on others. The next person after the Lord should be our spouse. Married people should love and honor their spouse above every other person.

An appropriate heart attitude for marriage is filled with love for God and love for one's spouse. A spiritual heart is regularly looking for ways to express those commitments. Motivated by integrity, honesty, respect, and faithfulness, a heart seeking God focuses on what is righteous and holy. It is a heart of love, godliness, trustworthiness, dependability, selflessness, and steadfast faithfulness. It remembers to whom we belong.

A heart that seeks the Lord is controlled by the Holy Spirit and exhibits the fruit of the Spirit. The characteristics are love, joy, peace, patience, kindness, goodness, faithfulness, gentleness, and self-control (Galatians 5:22–23). These are the hallmarks of a life surrendered to the Lord. The intentional choice should be to live life with these actions, even in circumstances when the human desire is the opposite.

Practically, this means choosing to act in love even when the other person is not being lovable or loving. It means choosing joy in the midst of turmoil, choosing to be peacemakers (not peacekeepers) in the midst of conflict; choosing to be patient when others are impatient; choosing kindness when others are mean, goodness in the face of evil, faithfulness when you want to give up, gentleness when others are harsh, and self-control when emotions feel out of control. This honors God and blesses the marriage.

The difference between peacemakers and peacekeepers is

the object and motivation of the heart. Jesus Christ called us to be peacemakers in the Sermon on the Mount. (Matthew 5:9) A peacemaker cares about the other person and brings positive resolution to conflicts. A peacekeeper focuses on self with a personal desire to avoid conflict at all costs. This usually comes at a very high cost to the relationship.

Thoughts and decisions lead to actions that reveal the heart. A disciplined thought life is a defense in living for Christ. Undisciplined thinking causes vulnerability to temptations. Controlling one's mind is difficult and must be intentional. It helps prevent negative and sinful thoughts from taking root.

> May the words of my mouth
>   and the meditation of my heart
>   be pleasing in your sight,
>   O LORD, my Rock and my Redeemer.
>   (Psalm 19:14)

In marriage, a husband guards his heart by guarding his eyes and purity. This means that he looks away from other women, in movies when necessary, from TV scenes or billboards that are inappropriate and when tempted to look at another woman. Additionally, he is not enthralled by the flattery or attention of other women toward him. He has committed to loving, honoring and respecting his wife and holds her in high esteem over all others.

> It is God's will that you should be sanctified:
>   that you should avoid sexual immorality.
>   (1 Thessalonians 4:3)

In marriage a wife can guard her heart by focusing only on her husband. She does this by not dressing, speaking, or acting in ways to catch the attention of other men. She is not interested in or responsive to other men's compliments and flirtations. She chooses to love, honor, and respect her own husband and acts with integrity and purity to give confidence to him.

Cleo and Sophia both said they wanted to guard their hearts and protect their marriage. However, the trust was unstable. Sophia was apprehensive of Cleo's previous habit of disrespectfully looking at other women. Then Cleo began to be disciplined in Bible reading and prayer. Sophia began to see a different attitude and deeper commitment to her. His actions gave her fresh, meaningful hope. The result was devotion to each other, and new strength in the marriage.

Commitment

Marriage is created by God and is sacred above all other earthly relationships. The starting point of protecting a marriage is commitment. In Christian marriages, commitment is made to the Lord and between the two marriage partners. It begins at the wedding and is reaffirmed many times throughout the marriage. The strongest marriages are built on God and the Bible as the foundation.

Commitment is a promise to stay pure and devoted to the spouse above all others. If a marriage is floundering, it is necessary to renew the commitment. If trust has been harmed in a marriage, the spoken promise that "I will not do those actions again" is critical. "I will be trustworthy, holy, and righteous and will live to prove this" is a necessary pledge for a marriage to have hope for the future.

The commitment in marriage is the understanding that in spite of difficulties and struggles, the couple will seek the Lord, be partners, and overcome problems. The steadfast promise to the marriage is a strong foundation in difficult times. When confidence is broken, the commitment wavers. Renewed obedience to the

Lord and His guidelines for marriage is the best way to reestablish genuine commitment.

The husband and wife are to be united in a relationship of oneness. This "oneness" is more creative, glorious, and meaningful that we can begin to imagine. Its plan is straight from the heart of God. There is no other relationship like it in the world. When a couple seeks the Lord and His Word to understand how to grow in oneness, wonderful joy abounds.

David and Leslie would describe their marriage as insecure. Historically, they have been reactionary to each other. Negative threats and actions provoke the same in return. Consequently, each doubts the commitment of the other, even though they say they are committed and want to be devoted. Years of retaliation have made them fearful. Recently, they have been challenged to confess to each other and trust God in a new, strong way. These decisions have been giant steps for them. The Lord is giving new and welcomed assurances.

Attitudes toward Others

What is the biblical attitude toward other relationships? In 1 Timothy 5:1–2, Paul counsels Timothy about how he should relate to others. This is a good model for marriages today as well. Paul tells Timothy that he should relate to men as if they were his father or his brother. He was instructed to relate to women as his mother or sisters, "with absolute purity." The passage teaches that purity is the goal.

> Do not rebuke an older man harshly, but exhort him as if he were your father. Treat younger men as brothers, older women as mothers, and younger women as sisters, with absolute purity. (1 Timothy 5:1–2)

Understanding the appropriate ways to relate to others outside the marriage clarifies the protective guidelines. Even in marriages where there has never been any broken trust, commitments need to be made based on defensive principles. In marriages with broken trust or unfaithfulness, strong barriers are essential to defend against future improprieties. Only in a shielded marriage is there hope of restored trust.

The attitudes of spouses are as important as the actions and applications of boundaries for the marriage. Both spouses must realize the importance of appropriate guidelines and be fully invested in carrying them out in practical ways. When one spouse feels the burden of being the main guardian of the marriage, it is exhausting, discouraging and overwhelming. If that spouse has to convince and persuade the other, then the heavy load can lead to wanting to give up.

If the unfaithful spouse in any way implies, "This is too hard," "This is too much to expect of me," or "Why is this important?" the whole process of restoration is uncertain. There are important things at stake. An attitude of commitment and all-in participation is needed. Otherwise, confidence crashes again. Trust repeatedly broken is more difficult to rebuild after every time.

It is not the faithful spouse's responsibility to carry the load to be proactive about establishing boundaries. It is the offending spouse's obligation to be convincing about a willing and sincere recommitment to the marriage in every protective way.

Cynthia and Robert are enjoying marital renewal. They were encouraged to apply 1 Timothy 5:1–2 to their marriage. They have committed to think of people differently and to change bad habits. Pervasive attitudes of flirtation, compromise, and indiscretion have been replaced with attitudes of honoring God and honoring each other by thinking of others differently. They have established new, protective guidelines, and their marriage is feeling the positive effects.

Personality

Often a person will describe himself or herself as having a "friendly (or outgoing) personality." Sometimes it is said with a wink and a spark of pride. "That's how God made me" is a favorite justification for patterns of relating to people of the opposite sex in ways that are too presumptuous. In reality, it is often a big excuse for inappropriate teasing and trespassing in relationships. The false premise is that flirty demeanor is acceptable.

The "outgoing" individual may act as if every person to whom he or she is flirtatious should feel lucky to have received the attention. He or she thinks others want the playful overtures and uninvited friendliness. It probably has not occurred to this spiritually immature "personality" that disrespectful and intrusive behaviors are unwelcome to the wise and discerning. This self-absorbed heart is out of touch with what is appropriate discretion.

The truth is that God gave personalities when He created us. However, the Lord never intended that we twist something good He gave us to become an excuse to sin against Him and others. Friendliness should be about treating all people with respect, kind consideration, and good boundaries. Personalities are not meant to justify inconsiderate behaviors that feed sinful idolatries. They are to be positive and wholesome in relationships, not harmful or disrespectful in any way.

Timothy and Lucy disagree about how to relate to others outside their marriage. Lucy likes being the "life of the party." She enjoys the laughter of men in response to her comments and jokes. Timothy has asked her to stop the friendliness with other men. However, she continues to flirt, defending her "friendly personality." Timothy has talked with her several times about changing her interactions. Nothing is changing. Lucy is blind to Timothy's heartache and loss of hope.

Social Media

Social media can be adversarial to marriages and stand as a major source of unfaithfulness, showing no partiality. Marriages need to have clear restrictions to protect them from social media. This is one area where passivity can be a gateway for destruction. It is a field teeming with temptations and dangers. When unsuspecting individuals participate without necessary wisdom, they can be tripped up very easily.

> Discretion will protect you,
>> and understanding will guard you.
> (Proverbs 2:11)

Unless a marriage takes steps to shield and put protections in place, potential harm can creep in and catch an unsuspecting couple with devastation. The naive or unaware can be swept away. Complacency is not acceptable. The enemy is beguiling and unrelenting. The world is resourceful and tenacious. Diligence and wisdom are of upmost importance. Minimizing the alarms is shortsighted. Each spouse needs to be committed to proactive protection.

There is a great deal at risk in this area. Every year, thousands of marriages are destroyed by problems that develop from use of the social media. Social media can multiply options and possibilities for secrecy and sinfulness. Commitments need to be clear and adhered to between marriage partners. It is not enough for spouses to just assume that they are in agreement about what's appropriate and best. It is important for a couple to discuss specifics so they can avoid pitfalls.

Here are some of the necessary guidelines:

- No spouse should be on any form of social media without the other spouse knowing about it.

- All passwords and keys should be completely disclosed to the spouse.
- Both spouses should have complete access to each other's social media accounts.
- There should not be personal communication with the opposite gender.
- No personal, emotional, marriage, or family information should be shared without the spouse's knowledge and agreement.
- If one spouse has a concern, the other spouse should honor any request for a change.

Lonnie and Dayna were nonchalant and dismissive of dangers and risks regarding social media. They casually dabbled in it but then became captivated and completely enthralled. No restrictions were in place. It was just a short time before enticements of unfaithfulness beckoned. They both fell prey before they were willing to admit what was happening. Their marriage was victimized and ravaged. Much damage happened very quickly. For them, the repair took months, for many other couples, it can even take years.

Friendships

Friendships are important to marriage. They can be a positive or a negative influence. There should be safeguards for marriage partners when it comes to friendships. The couple should be very careful to discuss guidelines regarding how each will relate to friends. It is important for men to build friendships with men and women to build friendships with women, even with other married couples.

Marriage partners should agree about friendships. The marriage should always be the priority over any friendship. If one spouse wants to continue a friendship against the other spouse's objection, this may indicate that the friendship is too important to that spouse. One spouse may feel uncomfortable about the other spouse's friend of the same gender or of the opposite gender for a variety of reasons.

If one spouse is uncertain about a friendship and its impacts on the marriage, he or she should express those feelings. The concern should not be dismissed or ignored. The other spouse should listen attentively, take steps to change behaviors, and defer to the spouse to work together so the worry is alleviated. This may involve ending the friendship. Each spouse should feel secure in the marriage. The spouses need to develop a plan to draw closer together, make each other a priority and act to protect the marriage.

Disregarding the distress is wrong and disrespectful to the spouse. Saying such things as "You are overreacting" or "You are just being too jealous" is unkind. There should be no defense of the outside relationship. Do not minimize the apprehension or justify inappropriate actions. The questioned spouse should respect the other's concerns. Take decisive steps. Realign with the spouse. However, if one spouse feels that the other spouse is being over sensitive, perhaps a counselor or minister could help them sort out what is appropriate.

> But among you there must not be even a hint of sexual immorality, or of any kind of impurity, or of greed, because these are improper for God's holy people. (Ephesians 5:3)

Sometimes a spouse, when confronted about not being guarded toward an outside person, may say, "Oh, I'm just being nice" or "I didn't want to hurt their feelings." These are not good answers. The spouse should stop the unwise interactions and not be more concerned about the friend than the spouse. Immediate behavior changes need to take place to honor the spouse.

When a spouse acts naively and minimizes potential harm from a lack of self-control, that person is living dangerously. God requires holiness. Hearts are filled with desires to rename sins and defend wrong choices. Marriages must be proactive and diligent in committing to holiness and honoring God in everything.

> Do not be misled: "Bad company corrupts good character." (1 Corinthians 15:33)

Edward and Betty moved into the neighborhood and wanted to get to know their neighbors. They began to have weekend cookouts. Previously they had been active in their church, but before long the Saturday nights lasted longer, and they were exhausted on Sunday mornings. Christian values, church attendance, and wholesome friends dropped off. Neighbor couples brought with them lots of alcohol and bad influences.

Soon poker games were added after the cookouts. Edward reluctantly agreed to non-betting games. However, the neighbors were pushy, Edward was weak, and soon money was involved. This encouraged more poker games to make up for losses from the week before. Edward did not call them off, even though they were happening in his game room. Betty begged him to stop, but the crowd was persuasive. Edward became disrespectful to Betty. The nice Edward she had married now acted like the neighbors.

Coworkers and Other Relationships

Marriage should be guarded in every setting. The workplace is often an environment where relationships can become inappropriate. Specific protective guidelines need to be in place and adhered to. We live in a culture that does not promote the sanctity of marriage and where unfaithfulness is common. There needs to be committed attentiveness to keep the marriage protected. Stand strong.

Christians should reflect characteristics of Jesus Christ. Such qualities as kindness and compassion often draw people like magnets. This can be detrimental without appropriate awareness.

A Christian needs to be cautious about being a listening ear or engaging in conversations that connect on an emotional and personal level with someone of the opposite gender. Things can develop quickly and are difficult to turn around.

Imagine if a woman comes up to a man in the office and begins to say, "You seem like such a nice man. You are a good father, and I think you're probably a good husband. I wish I had a good husband like you. My husband is selfish and doesn't care about me." Immediately, the man is at an important decision position. He can choose to deflect the inviting conversation with a wise and kind response, or he can choose to be enticed by her statements. It is important that he act wisely.

Even a simple response of "Thank you. Sorry to hear that about your marriage. You deserve a good marriage" is already too engaging and can easily be misconstrued. A better response would be "What you're telling me is very important, but I'm not the person to hear this. I would encourage you to talk to _____. She is a loving Christian woman in our office."

What if a man approaches a female coworker and says, "You look great today, as always. I appreciate how you take care of yourself physically and dress in becoming ways. You're the best-looking woman in this office. I wish my wife would take care of herself like you do"? That woman has to quickly decide what she is going to do with his uninvited flattery. Will she enjoy his flirtation or will she respond appropriately to end his come-ons?

"Thank you for noticing. I was hoping I was making a good impression" would not be a right response. She can respectfully say, "Our relationship is to be only professional. Please do not talk about my appearance." Perhaps she does need to evaluate how she is dressing and presenting herself. Should she notch up the modesty to ward off such comments?

Both of these examples and others happen often in the work world. It is important for people to be prepared for such attention. Many times, when caught off guard, one can find it difficult to respond in the best way. Human nature enjoys flattery so one should always be on guard.

Even with relatives, spouses need to act with discretion and respect. Sometimes familiar relationships cause hedges to be lowered. Feeling comfortable and connected can bring about a closeness that invites teasing, touching, and transferring emotions to someone outside the marriage but possibly inside the family. History of knowing each other and appreciating strengths can suddenly seem to develop into wrong feelings and actions. In all relationships, both family ties and friendships, the predetermined decision of faithfulness must never diminish.

The Bible, in Leviticus 18:1–30, goes into specific detail about warnings and guidelines for family relationships on many levels. There should be persistent and intentional care to guard them in every way. God wants each family relationship to be treated with respect and protection. He instructs righteous and trustworthy actions. Family relationships can become relaxed, casually removing discernment. It is heartbreaking to hear of affairs within families.

Andrea could testify to that. Her husband, Bradley, had an affair with her sister, Joan. The slippery slope began with teasing and jesting. He began to seek her out with private conversations. Things happened quickly, and suddenly they realized they had fallen into an adulterous affair. Even though they both chose to end it quickly, the damage was done. Andrea caught them alone in the house together. The affair brought immense sadness, strife, and ongoing complications to the family for years to come. It all could and should have been avoided.

Personal Space

Marriage is designed by God to share personal space in oneness. That does not mean that there has to be constant touch, but it does mean that there are no boundaries. We are in the same "space" as our spouse, where touch and loving affection should be a very important component of any marriage. In a marriage, all space can be shared space, but that is not true in other relationships.

Discretion reveals commitment to integrity. Appropriate discretion avoids being alone with someone of the opposite gender outside the marriage. Even when it seems innocent, safeguards still need to be in place. This includes business appointments when at all possible, involving meals and riding in cars, etc. The point is to diminish temptation and avoid appearance of any wrong. When unavoidable, keep the conversation impersonal, and talk about your spouse in the most favorable manner.

Even when a spouse is not present, a married person should always act in a way that honors God and honors his or her spouse. Understanding and applying principles for personal space is a "circumference of commitment." The cliché of "standing at arm's length" is actually a good principle. A married person should position himself or herself at a careful distance from anyone of the opposite gender. Be alert when others try to breach the distance.

Steven has always treated other women in all settings with a polite distance. From the beginning of his marriage with Sylvia he told her that he loves her above every other woman and wants to make sure they know that. Steven has a kind heart but doesn't cross the line with any woman to talk personally or engage in private conversations. He graciously talks about Sylvia to others. His physical touch, meaningful glances, and loving words are only for her. He is known for his integrity and respected by others.

Words

When married, spouses need to change how they talk to people outside the marriage. Words have great impact and need to show clear discretion. No information should be shared with others outside of the marriage that sparks emotions or stirs feelings inappropriately.

If you are experiencing struggles and heartbreak within your marriage share it only with objective godly people who can provide positive impact to help bring necessary changes. This may be a minister or a Biblical counselor. There should be no negative, disparaging or derogatory talk about the marriage or one's spouse.

Sexual communication outside marriage is inappropriate. To invite or engage in sexual exchanges, jokes, or innuendoes is improper and should be avoided. Though it may appear innocent or insignificant at first, it is wrong and destructive. In work settings, neighborhoods, and friendships, things may be communicated in an enticing way. Do not get hooked in. Get yourself out of any destructive e-mail chain.

Be alert, and exhibit great discernment toward what gets a quick laugh or turns a head. Care unrelentingly about what is good and pure and honors God. Choose to be fully committed to the Lord and to your spouse. Put safeguards in place to guard your heart. Stand up for what is right, and confront what is wrong.

Wrong scenarios can begin quickly and insidiously. Say "No!" to every temptation that dishonors God and violates your spouse. Make decisions to turn away, stop communication, go a different direction, take a stand, or change patterns so as not to become involved in private secret communication with anyone.

No communication should connect emotionally in a personal way with someone outside your marriage. Sweet words should be saved only for a spouse. Praise, flattery, teasing, flirting, sarcasm, and even negative banter that solicits a response from a person outside the marriage are all precarious. Shared interests, similarities, or differences can be manipulated to engage someone in interaction. Do a heart check. Avoid all speech that can lower your guard and lead to sinful actions.

In the same way, a married person should not be easily taken in by flattery, affirmation, engaging questions, advice seeking, or any method used to connect with ego or emotions. Be discerning of accolades. Protecting marriage necessitates being on guard and living with clear boundaries. It is easy to be caught unsuspecting with an ego pull.

Lance and Emily know firsthand about the importance of saying things in right ways. Both are comfortable in conversation and think of themselves as affirmers. However, Lance has learned the hard way about the consequence of friendly conversation with women. A new couple began to visit the church. Trying to make them feel welcome, Lance encouraged their attendance. The other woman took it personally and began to call and text him after she found his number in the class directory. Eventually he had to change his number to stop it.

Physical Touch

Be careful about any touch toward or from someone of the opposite gender outside of marriage. "Keep your hands to yourself" is still a good mandate. Touching, poking, patting, kissing, and hugging are generally improper and can be easily misunderstood by your spouse and others. Even between relatives there needs to be a high standard of limited touch. Everything should respect the spouse, even when he or she is not present.

Do nothing that hurts your spouse or invites or pursues others. Hugging should be avoided or be minimal or sideways with someone outside the marriage. Even when others are insistent on hugging in a more personal way, change things. It takes two to hug. Substitute a handshake or step back. Communicate respectfully, either with or without words, that you are not a hugger. As you act with discretion, others usually adjust.

Unity as a Couple

Be seen together as a couple. Interact together as a pair whenever possible. Do things jointly in many ways. Be a united front. This will strengthen the marriage and be a source of enjoyment for the marriage partners. Time spent together increases closeness and appreciation for each other. It builds accountability and pleasure in the marriage. It also proclaims to others the marriage devotion.

Being a strong unit as a couple protects the marriage. Block outside distractions, and build an impenetrable team. Let your marriage be visibly united at the heart. Safeguarding your marriage is enhanced with each measure and action that you do together. Talk about your spouse favorably to others. Treat your spouse lovingly in front of others.

Friends describe Donald and Elyse as inseparable. That hasn't always been true. For the first fifteen years of their marriage, they were seldom seen together. After a near affair between Elyse and a man in her fitness class, she felt the wake-up call. Recommitting to her marriage and more activities with Donald has produced a surprise. Being intentional to do more together has resulted in great enjoyment and a renewed marriage. Donald and Elyse have fun together now and love their shared events.

Benefits of Protecting Marriage

Protecting your marriage is an imperative goal. Even marriages that have not experienced broken trust need to be committed to preserving and strengthening the trust. Meticulous attention toward fortifying your marriage is wise and necessary. After a marriage has struggled with broken trust, standing guard over it is absolutely vital.

Precaution and prevention are two essential characteristics for a dedicated and steadfast marriage. Ignoring the need to guard a marriage is irresponsible and naïve. Nonchalance and apathy are dangerous. Striving to have the strongest marriage possible requires forethought, a careful plan, and the fortitude to implement it consistently. The marriage then enjoys energized trust, security, confidence, and oneness.

Ignoring the need to guard a marriage is irresponsible and

naive. Nonchalance and apathy are dangerous. Guard the marriage with vigilance, recognizing its significance. Your marriage is worth the highest level of promise and protection. Securing marriage treats it with the priceless value that Jesus Christ ordained it to have. Honor and obey the Lord by treasuring your marriage as the precious relationship that God created it to be.

14

Investing in Your Marriage

But store up for yourselves treasures in heaven, where moths
and rust do not destroy, and where thieves do not break in and
steal. For where your treasure is, there your heart will be also.
—Matthew 6:20–21

A study by Northwestern Mutual Insurance Company revealed
that half of Americans have no financial plan for investing for the
future. This research discovered that 63 percent of Americans said
that their financial plan needs improvement. The respondents in
this study said that the number-one obstacle for their lack of an
investment plan is not having enough time.[2] More important than
a financial plan for investing in the future is an intentional plan
to invest in the quality of your marital relationship.

Marriages should be valued. When trust has been broken or
harmed in a marriage, it is even more important. A new start
should include significant ways of meaningfully pouring back into
the marriage. Investing in your marriage intentionally targets
specific areas for the maximum benefit for healing, growth, restored
trust, and blessings. It takes time and effort to invest in marriage
adequately. It deserves your best.

Investing in marriage means honoring it as a great priority.
Focusing on the relationship of marriage with efforts and

commitments that will positively affect the other spouse is foundational for strengthening marriage. Make life-changing contributions that will have ongoing influence in the marriage; this will bring rich dividends. To treasure something means to recognize its value and know it is precious.

Time together and shared experiences strengthen love, marital satisfaction and trust. Safeguarding your marriage is enhanced with each commitment and action that you do together. Looking for new experiences in a variety of areas as a couple enriches the union. Do things as a team. Participating in activities together helps you learn about each other and develop stronger bonds. Friendship in marriage is a deep source of joy.

Investing from the resources that God has given to creatively highlight the value of marriage and one's spouse, pays off with abundant joy. It is worth the cost, and involvement. Commit to more sacrificial love and less selfishness. Communicate in many ways to your spouse about all he or she means to you. Let your actions support your words. The blessings that God will bring, and the appreciation that your spouse will feel, will reap meaningful returns with far reaching gains.

Invest Spiritually

Marriage is a spiritual union. It is a covenant between a man, a woman, and God. God created and consecrated marriage. He established and ordained the guiding principles. The only way a marriage can truly be all that it was designed to be is if God is the central focus. A husband and wife experience God's richest blessings as they place Him as the Lord of their relationship.

Establishing spiritual disciplines as a couple strengthens and guides the marriage. Some of these spiritual disciplines include Bible reading, prayer, worship, service, and ministry. Each of these can have a unique impact on the marriage and add depth and joy.

The disciplines are not the goal. Rather, they are the results of a deeply committed love for the Lord Jesus Christ. Relationship with the Lord is a response to His outpouring of love for us.

It is with gratitude from a transformed heart that we respond to God. When a marriage is devoted to Jesus Christ, it has the greatest possibility for strength and hope. Couples who love God and want to honor Him in their marriages can experience His indescribable power and love for them. It is amazing to realize that a heart that loves God and seeks to know Him more deeply can inspire simple disciplines as a couple that can bring greater blessings and meaningful results.

Read the Bible Individually and Together

> All Scripture is God-breathed and is useful for teaching, rebuking, correcting and training in righteousness. (2 Timothy 3:16)

The Bible is God's Word. It is God-inspired and given for teaching, rebuking, correcting, and teaching in righteousness. It includes instructions for relationships and for life. God's design for marriage is revealed in the Bible. Reading the Bible and discussing it together as a couple is a very special way of growing together. It is encouraging to understand that God's Word is practical and filled with relevant, life-changing truths. The Bible also comforts in times of difficulties and grief.

> Do not merely listen to the Word, and so deceive yourselves. Do what it says. Anyone who listens to the Word but does not do what it says is like a man who looks at his face in a mirror and, after looking at himself, goes away and immediately forgets what he looks like. (James 1:22-24)

God's Word is truth. It provides wisdom for everything we face in life. The Bible is a light into our heart revealing areas of sin and needed growth. It also inspires to do what is right. When we study God's Word, it is important that we apply the truths we find there. Otherwise it is like looking in a mirror and then forgetting what we look like.

God's relationship with mankind and design for marriage are more creative and wonderful than anyone can describe. God's awesome principles are life-changing. When couples are committed to knowing God's Word and applying its truths in their lives, they can experience wonderful strength, happiness and resulting oneness.

Jesus taught that hearing and putting God's Word into practice is like building a house on a solid foundation. Applying biblical truths in everyday life gives strength in times of struggles. When storms come, the Bible helps a couple weather through with peace. Difficulties and trials come to every marriage and family. The best way to be prepared for the tough times in life is to be established in God's Word. The Bible gives practical instructions, examples, comfort, and encouragement for trying times.

> I will show you what he is like who comes to me and hears my words and puts them into practice. He is like a man building a house, who dug down deep and laid the foundation on rock. When a flood came, the torrent struck that house but could not shake it, because it was well built. But the one who hears my words and does not put them into practice is like a man who built a house on the ground without a foundation. The moment the torrent struck that house, it collapsed and its destruction was complete. (Luke 6:47–49)

Kevin and Leesa did not grow up in Christian homes and felt lacking in their biblical knowledge after they became Christians.

Some Christian friends began to meet with them to read the Bible and encouraged them to read it as a couple. Before long they became more familiar with Bible stories and passages. They say, "We never realized how much we were missing or how amazing the Bible is. It's refreshing and encouraging and gives answers to life's problems." It has brought a new closeness to their marriage.

Pray with and for Your Spouse

Prayer is an amazing miracle. Prayer is talking to God and listening to Him. To think that we can engage in conversation at any time about anything with the almighty God of the universe is mind-boggling. The second equally marvelous thought is that God Himself desires our conversation and wants a close personal relationship with us. In fact, He beckons us to Himself with the most extraordinary invitation for forgiveness and salvation.

> The eyes of the Lord are on the righteous,
>   and his ears are attentive to their cry.
> (Psalm 34:15)

God intended prayer to be a significant component of marriage. Prayer allows marriage partners to enter the presence of God united and open to His guidance. Prayer is simply talking to God about anything and everything. It is one of the sweetest, most intimate experiences that a husband and wife can share.

God, through prayer, gives wisdom and direction for decisions in life. None of us can face the challenges and questions that come without relying on the Lord for leadership, encouragement, and hope. Even if praying as a couple can feel awkward at first, it is very important to begin together in simple conversations with God.

Praying with and for your spouse is very meaningful. To ask "How can I pray for you?" endears spouses to each other in a special way. When a wife is asked if she would like to pray with her husband, the usual response is "Yes. That would mean so much to me!" Praying together gives a wife security in knowing that her husband is seeking God's guidance.

Worship

The call to worship is a theme of the Bible from beginning to end. Worship is a privilege and a responsibility for every person. God created every person to worship God. We are drawn to worship God because He alone is worthy of our praise and adoration. Worship focuses our minds and hearts on God, the creator and sustainer of the universe. It reminds us of the majesty of our Savior and king, all He has done for us, and how much we need Him.

> Let us hold unswervingly to the hope we profess, for he who promised is faithful. And let us consider how we may spur one another on toward love and good deeds, not giving up meeting together, as some are in the habit of doing, but encouraging one another—and all the more as you see the Day approaching. (Hebrews 10:23–25)

The Bible instructs that we should regularly worship with other believers. Christians should encourage one another to continue to grow in their faith. Worshipping turns our hearts toward the greatness of the Lord. It reminds us of His goodness and how we belong to Him. Praise and worship express gratitude, thanksgiving, and surrender to God. Worship restores joy in our walk with the Lord and creates a community of fellowship with other believers.

Ministry and Service Together

Ministering as a couple provides deep enjoyment and satisfaction for your marriage. Finding an area in which you can serve together allows you to blend your spiritual gifts and be a blessing to others. Many times spouses serve individually, but it is an even more fulfilling experience to find some areas to serve as a couple. This increases your impact and bonds your hearts together. It is lots of fun and enlightening to realize and utilize your spiritual gifts together.

Each believer is given spiritual gifts at the time of salvation. These are given to serve the body of Christ in the church and to share the gospel with nonbelievers. There are many assessments and tools to help determine a person's spiritual gifts. If you don't know your spiritual gifts, check into some ways to evaluate that. Talk to other Christians who know you well about what they think are your spiritual gifts. You might be surprised and encouraged by what you learn.

Married couples who serve and minister together grow in their relationship with Jesus Christ. It provides an opportunity to be like the "hands and feet" of the Lord to do service for others. It sets an example for family members and children about the blessings of obeying the Lord. Finding a place of service provides a way to express the joy experienced in relationship with the Lord and to show the love of Jesus Christ.

Christian ministry is different from community projects. The difference is the message of Jesus Christ. Wanting to be involved in areas of ministry in the communities is based on the realization that people need the Lord. We are compelled to share the good news of God's truth, love, and forgiveness. Jesus instructed believers to care for those in need around us. Serving is one of the most fulfilling aspects of a Christian's life and enjoyable for couples together.

Mary and Harvey had experienced strained times throughout their marriage. Off and on, they felt detached from each other. Both wanted to experience closer emotional intimacy and increase their shared interests. Different recreational preferences and hobbies resulted in time apart and disconnection. As Harvey was expressing this to their pastor one day, the pastor suggested they try to find an area of service or ministry that they could do together. They began to reach out to newcomers in the community. Over time, it became a true blessing for the church and a wonderful joy for their marriage.

Invest Emotionally

Emotional investment in a marriage is worthwhile. If a marriage is healthy and strong emotionally, it feels happy and fulfilling with joy and confidence. If it is emotionally weak it feels deficient and lonely. Investing in the emotional health of your marriage is a wise and important commitment. Emotional intimacy produces positive feelings of oneness in marriage, while emotional voids cause spouses to feel like roommates.

The description of emotionally healthy marriages often seems ambiguous and illusive. However, the subjective reporting of an emotionally hurting marriage is clear and specific. A spouse can quickly describe many areas of sadness and disconnection. The degree of emotional health and stability in the marriage is a consistent factor in reporting satisfaction. Moving toward the relationship intentionally with caring and consideration helps a spouse feel cherished. These are strong descriptors of a happy marriage.

Positive Communication

Positive communication is one of the largest contributors toward a healthy marriage. It is often one of the major characteristics mentioned in a positive, happy marriage, or in a negative way for unhappy marriages. Marital health has a direct correlation with how respectful the communication is between the spouses. Many times, spouses report that with everyone else, they view themselves as a positive communicator. However, with their spouse, they feel that communication is discouraging and frustrating.

The encouraging word is that communication is a learned skill. Communication has huge potential for growth and capacity for change in a marriage. Individuals can improve in communication and couples can learn to communicate better together. The relationship can undergo encouraging growth if there is willingness to change patterns and harmful habits. Couples get excited as they begin to see their marriage changing. The love for each other, the feeling of being understood, and the experience of a deeper level of respect can be invigorating.

Every effort made in a marriage to learn to listen well, care about the other's feelings, lower the volume to calm emotions, discuss issues with a desire to resolve them in a loving way, and ask for forgiveness when wrong is a step toward a more God-honoring relationship. The outcome is worth the effort every time. Immense and long-lasting blessings bring comfort, deeper commitment, and a more hopeful future for a marriage. The desire to grow in communication replenishes the marriage.

To express affirmation and appreciation in marriage is to make unique contributions. Spouses need to remember and express often what they appreciate about each. Consistently looking for things to express thanksgiving for in one another helps each one feel loved and valued. Big things and little things deserve recognition and acknowledgement. Looking for things to praise, building each other up, and encouraging one another are healthy patterns that strengthen and protect a marriage. Take regular opportunities to communicate to your spouse how special he or she is to you.

Joseph and Betsy were both quiet and reserved. Conversations between them were meager and emotions not adequately expressed. They often felt disconnected and lonely in the marriage. It was suggested that they express appreciation and affirmation for each other every day. Tepidly at first, and then more confidently, they began to affirm and express thanksgiving for each other. They grew closer, felt more cared for by each other, and displayed more happiness. They each described a beautiful breakthrough and new, rich blessings in their marriage.

Investing in marriage also means resolving conflicts as they come up. Issues need to be addressed in a timely way and by using positive methods. Though emotions may be intense, the commitment must be to treat each other respectfully even when upset. The Bible has many practical instructions for communicating and solving differences. It is crucial to not sin in anger (Ephesians 4:26), to use wholesome words (Ephesians 4:29), to keep the volume under control (Proverbs 15:1), and to speak the truth in love (Ephesians 4:15).

Stay Connected

Purposeful communication with lots of conversation is vital to a healthy and vibrant marriage. It draws the partners closer together. Commit to resolve issues as they come up and stay current about concerns. Conversation is important to both spouses. It is generally agreed that as much as husbands desire physical intimacy, wives desire meaningful conversation. The commitment of intentional conversation with each other every day is one of the sweetest gifts spouses can give to each other.

In early marriage my husband gave a very special blessing to me that has lasted for decades. He offered to have meaningful conversation every day to talk about anything I wanted to talk about for as long as I desired. We began having daily talk times with no distractions. Very soon it became apparent that we both enjoyed it and needed it. Now at the end of each day my husband will still often take the lead saying, "Ready to talk?" This commitment has contributed to the sweetness and tenderness in our marriage.

Contact each other during the day to communicate that you

are thinking of each other. Call, text or e-mail. Be available, if possible, to listen when one needs to talk. Look forward to seeing each other at the end of a day. Plan together and capitalize on daily talk times at the end of the day to debrief from the day. Express your affection for each other, and look for new and creative ways to show your love.

Claire and Connor were young executives with demanding jobs. Computers, smartphones, online meetings, and conference calls filled their lives. Professional busyness permeated the marriage. Evenings were times together but on their devices. Preoccupation with their phones and iPads had taken precedence over personal dialogue. One night Claire texted Connor and invited him to meet on the sofa for a real conversation with no distractions. It felt refreshing. That started a promise to each other to put away devices at night and concentrate on each other. This has revitalized their marriage.

Intentional motivation from both spouses toward the marriage is respectful and loving. If one spouse feels the heavy load of being the one who is trying to stay connected and increase the emotional investment, it is discouraging and frustrating. If one spouse has to encourage a partner to make time for the marriage, to take one's share of the responsibilities, or to engage in events and conversation to help grow and strengthen the relationship, it feels emotionally exhausting. The root cause of relational laziness is prideful selfishness. It beats up the trust in marriage. No persuasion can force a change in someone's heart. It comes from commitment and sacrificial love.

Serve Each Other

> You, my brothers and sisters, were called to be free. But do not use your freedom to indulge the flesh; rather, serve one another humbly in love. (Galatians 5:13)

Imagine a marriage in which each spouse strives to out-serve the other. Looking for opportunities to lighten each other's load brings delight and sweet relief to the marriage. Being aware of difficulties your spouse faces and looking for specific and personal ways to encourage have ripple effects of deep appreciation and gratitude. Simple acts like jumping up to help carry in groceries, cleaning a bathroom unexpectedly, polishing shoes, washing a car, doing the dishes, and folding clean clothes all communicate a heart of love and service.

These actions endear spouses to each other. Sacrificial serving and commitment show untiring love. If this is a new concept in your marriage, surprise your spouse. Set the example, and be the first to realize that you are doing something so near to the heart of God. Invigorating joy rolls back onto the spouse who understands and enjoys the privilege of serving. Serving has a way of recalibrating the marriage back to a positive place. It leads to holiness in marriage.

Emotional intimacy is enhanced when responsibilities and tasks are shared. Serving each other in marriage helps carry the load and draws you close as a team. Be attentive in caring and showing sacrificial love through service for each other. Find ways to help each other daily. Share responsibilities. Try to out-serve each other. Follow up when you say you will do something. Look for ways to bless each other by doing more than expected or anticipated.

Each person should carry one's own responsibilities and also work together for joint tasks. There are some chores and responsibilities that are delegated to each spouse. Others are to be shared, working together to accomplish them. In Galatians 6:2, it says to carry each other's burdens. In Galatians 6:5, we are taught to carry our own load. A comparison can be that personal responsibilities are like a backpack and carrying each other's burdens involves bigger jobs that require carrying them together.

> Carry each other's burdens, and in this way you
> will fulfill the law of Christ ... for each one should
> carry his own load. (Galatians 6:2, 5)

Invest Relationally

Developing Christ-honoring friendships is a good way to invest in your marriage. Putting forth the effort to get to know other couples and develop friendships with couples who are like-minded in faith can be enjoyable and beneficial. Be discerning to select couples who genuinely love the Lord and have appropriate convictions and commitments, whose lives show integrity, trustworthiness, and purity.

Form friendships with Christian couples that are growing in their Christian walk. They can be positive encouragers. These couples should be carefully chosen with prayer and observation of their lives first. Evaluate their actions, love for God, and commitment to each other. Look for a godly Christian couple who show positive characteristics in their own marriage.

Both spouses should be involved in choosing a couple as friends. If either spouse has a hesitancy about a certain couple, then they should not seek a close friendship with that couple. Look for another couple about whom you both feel good and can agree. Listen, and respect your spouse's feelings. Even in Christian couples, each person should always maintain appropriate boundaries, with careful discernment and commitment to the Lord and to one's spouse.

Laura and Richard were trying to invest in their marriage. They agreed to develop some Christian friends. In their Bible study class, they met Michelle and Alan, who have a good marriage, are authentic believers in Jesus Christ, and are not materialistic or competitive as other couples are. The two couples have enjoyed some dinners together, and Laura and Richard hope the friendship can continue. For the first time in their marriage they have friends that encourage them to grow in their faith as a couple.

Always consult with your spouse before making any plans and commitments with anyone else. Talk with your spouse, checking calendars and agreeing on priorities. This even includes plans with family members. Be diligent to give the priority to your spouse showing love and respect. Honor each other above all others. Be sensitive to each other to know what activities and events are important to one another.

Invest Financially

Celebrate Special Events

Life is full of important and memorable events. Add to that the significant relationships and experiences that matter, and you have many occasions to celebrate in life. Every person deserves and appreciates recognition. Seek opportunities to give applause and say, "You are precious to me." It is worth the time, expense, and effort. Even capitalizing on simple, happy ways of showing and expressing "I love you!" can make for unexpected sweet surprises. They build up emotional investments that dance in the hearts and minds of loved ones for a long time.

The results from expressing love are more valuable even than the investment. Sometimes the cost is actually minimal, but the returns are rich rewards. Writing a poem to confirm one's love because it's Tuesday, cleaning out a car to reward going the extra mile, putting a new book on Kindle to give someone personal time, and having the lawn professionally mowed so you both can go to a movie on Saturday—all signify deliberate attention and desire to honor and please.

Remember the old MasterCard commercials? They would show many different relationship events and ways that things could be purchased to gain something of great value. For example:

$49 for the fishing rod, $18 for the fishing license, time together = "priceless." Investing in marriage is similar, but actually on a much grander scale. Examples: $150 for the hotel, $100 for the conference, renewed marriage = "priceless"; $30 picnic dinner, $40 babysitter, a walk together in a park = "priceless"; $500 for the reception, $100 for the new dress, renewal of vows = "priceless".

Make Marriage Memories

Resources spent for romantic weekends away, anniversary gifts, vacations, and magical memories are all investments with long-lasting impacts. Gifts show connection and belonging together. They can also communicate desire for fresh starts and gratitude for forgiveness and second chances, commemorating new directions and renewed commitments. Money allotted for marriage vow renewals is often some of the best investment that a marriage can make. It reminds, refocuses, and repledges a husband and wife to each other for the rest of their lives. Sometimes when a marriage is restored after broken trust, vow renewal is deeply memorable.

Put forth the effort and energy to creatively plan for times together. The price tag is not what gives the value. Rather it is the gift of making it a priority and wanting to be together. Whether in your home with candles, a white tablecloth, and a store-bought dessert after the children are asleep; meeting for lunch while the children are in school so you don't have to pay for a babysitter; or taking a nice coffee to your spouse at work, each endeavor says, "You are important to me!" Find increments of time to turn into thoughtful messages of devotion. You did it when you were dating; now do it again.

Don't be stingy. Pray for wisdom to discern those important instances when planning something special is needed and right. Being too frugal can lead to missed opportunities and regrets. This does not mean being reckless or irresponsible stewards of your resources. However, usually there can be some money designated for something meaningful. Celebrate life. Celebrate each other. Celebrate your marriage, a gift from the Lord. Invest in memories.

Jack and Natalie were working to get their marriage back on track and to grow closer together. Jack had been unfaithful, and Natalie found out. He confessed and said he wanted to repent completely. She was willing to give him a chance to do that. They had talked together about a second honeymoon trip to renew their vows. They planned it for weeks, and then Jack seemed to cool to the idea and expressed concern about the cost. It was important to Natalie, but she shortened the trip to economize. Right after their trip, Natalie learned that Jack had planned a fishing trip with his buddies and had not told her. He already had the reservations when she found out. It was a crushing disappointment for Natalie to see Jack's blatant selfishness again. It was a setback for the marriage.

Invest Physically

Be Present and Attentive

There are important ways for spouses to be present and attentive to each other in marriage. Kindness and sensitivity to each other's feelings and desires are loving and vital for the union of two hearts in marriage.

Availability is making each other a priority so that at any time the needs of one's spouse rise to the top and override other needs. This comes with a keen awareness of each other's responsibilities, schedules, and demands. The willingness to walk alongside, being flexible to help and respond when needs increase, is very considerate. It says, "I love you and care about all you do." Genuine attentiveness toward a spouse is compassionate and greatly appreciated.

Schedule life and activities together as much as possible. This includes leisure times and recreational events. Sharing time doing chores together and then enjoyable leisure activities together are some of the most satisfying and fulfilling occasions in life. They bring a sense of accomplishment and satisfaction in the relationship. If they are not already established in the marriage, work as a team to invest in these areas.

Another way to be present together is in the daily scheduling of wake-up times and bedtimes together. This usually means some compromise and adjustment from both spouses because of schedules and preferences. Though this may sound unimportant, in reality, it contributes to marital oneness and a sense of being in sync and harmony together in the rhythm of life. The early morning times and the last hours and minutes of the day are considered some of the most relational time periods. Happier marriages interface these times together as much as possible.

Physical Intimacy

The biblical view is that physical intimacy and sexual activity belong only in the context of marriage between a man and a woman. God's gift of physical intimacy is to bless marriages in many ways. One of the main ways is for a spouse to be able to say to the other spouse, "I love you more than words can describe." Physical intimacy and sexual relations in marriage are amazing expressions of God's creativity and His love for us. They provide blessings of joy and pleasure that are personal, meaningful, grace-filled, and enriching to a marriage.

Every husband and wife should realize that the sexual drive that God placed in each person is good. It should only be satisfied in the context of their marriage. All other sexual activity is sin. Additionally, each spouse needs to understand that he or she is the only person on the face of the earth who has the privilege and responsibility of meeting the sexual needs and desires of his or her spouse. There are no other people or options.

There needs to be willingness and an eagerness to meet the spouse's needs. This means being intentional and available to your spouse to express physical love in a selfless and attentive way. All affection and sexual activity in marriage must be kind, respectful, loving, tender, understanding, gentle, and patient. Marriage affection can be playful, inviting, always respectful to your spouse and honoring to God's design.

Even when spouses are on different libido levels in the schedule of daily activities and life, the goal is to give a gift of love to your spouse that tenderly and respectfully says, "You are precious and I am committed to you." The giving and receiving of this gift of physical intimacy should be focused on being loving toward the other person. There is a big difference between "I love you" and "I love me and want you to do for me." Being available and not being demanding are two aspects of selfless love.

Physical Health

As a Christ follower, your body is the temple of God. The Bible teaches that we have a responsibility to live physically in obedience to God. As stewards of our physical body, we need to live with a larger focus than our personal desires and appetites.

> Therefore, I urge you, brothers, in view of God's mercy, to offer your bodies as living sacrifices, holy and pleasing to God—this is your spiritual act of worship. Do not conform any longer to the pattern of this world, but be transformed by the renewing of your mind. Then you will be able to test and approve what God's will is, his good, pleasing and perfect will. (Romans 12:1–2)

We are taught to offer our body as a living sacrifice to God. Our body is the vessel by which God allows for us to live for Him. Taking care of our body means protecting it to use for the glory of God. To surrender our body to live for Him is to give the most personal thing we can give. Physical responsibility is twofold: to do what is healthy and avoid what is harmful. As we turn from worldly views and renew our minds with a spiritual perspective, we understand what God's will is for us.

Another aspect of investing in your marriage is investing in your physical health. This adds to the quality of your life. Physical health determines how a person feels, how active one can be, and how fully one can participate in aspects of life. Many times our health is out of our control. However, we can strive toward some proven strategies that contribute to overall health and well-being. These commitments communicate love to a spouse because they show that one wants to be healthy and well for as long as possible. A healthy lifestyle should be a priority.

What we value, we take care of. If we value our health, we will take appropriate steps to protect it. Self-control and discipline are key foundational tools for making wise decisions regarding our health for a lifetime. Our health practices impact not just ourselves but also others who care about us. Educate yourself regarding good health, and make commitments to do the very best you can. Be motivated and responsible yourself. Don't make others feel the need to have to persuade you. Your life is worth it. Your spouse and family are worth your being healthy for them. God is certainly worth living a life that is holy and healthy for Him.

Steven and Phyllis had been married for four years and had become lax in healthy disciplines. Consequently, they both had put on weight, especially Steven. At his annual checkup, he learned that he had become diabetic and needed to change his lifestyle or go on insulin. They agreed to try and turn it around with exercise and diet. Working together, they began a disciplined regimen. Fortunately, he was able to make significant changes. He was surprised how much better he felt. He also began to understand that his body is the temple of God. The new surrender and commitment brought a turnaround for some of their priorities. Their marriage grew in greater appreciation, respect, and love.

Investing in marriage is a significant aspect of healthy marriages. It benefits strong and loving marriages and strengthens marriages that are seeking renewal and recommitment. In the Bible, God blessed and multiplied fishes and loaves that were given to Him. Similarly, the Lord blesses and multiplies marriage when the spouses invest in their marriage. The returns and benefits are usually much greater than the investments made. God always does more than we can imagine when we trust and obey Him.

15

The Importance of Trust

The man of integrity walks securely,
but he who takes crooked paths will be found out.
—Proverbs 10:9

A wife of noble character who can find?
She is worth far more than rubies.
Her husband has full confidence in her
and lacks nothing of value.
—Proverbs 31:10–11

Trust is foundational to marriage. A healthy marriage has strong trust, and in fact, a marriage cannot grow and be healthy without strong trust. God ordained and created marriage. God is trustworthy and wants the marriage relationship to be trustworthy. God proves Himself as trustworthy and instructs us to do the same as we relate to each other.

Trust is the assurance that a marriage partner will be reliable to engage in appropriate decisions and actions. Good character, convictions, and right values are the best principles that encourage respect and confidence in marriage. When a spouse has peace of mind that their partner will act faithfully in all circumstances, there is assurance and deep joy. Without marital confidence, uncertainty can quickly cause distrust.

Ambiguous trust causes uncertainty, dissatisfaction, and concern in every area of the marriage. Many times marriages struggle not because trust has been broken but because it is weak and tentative. Marriage despondency and instability bring decline in closeness and relational peace of mind. When this is the case, positive steps are needed to strengthen the confidence by building up the trust in the relationship. Each spouse should discuss concerns about trust, being honest about uncertainties.

When a spouse discusses feelings of despondency or uncertainty about the trust level in the marriage, they should be explored more deeply. Without carefully sorting through these feelings, listening, and taking positive actions to strengthen the trust, a spouse can feel unheard and devalued. Each spouse should seek to respond favorably to the other spouse's concerns and grow in trustworthiness. Be willing to assess, invest in building the marital trust with specific actions, and establish new patterns for positive change.

Trust building focuses on caring for the other person. Some spouses may say, "You just need to trust me." However, the focus should instead be on "I need to live in a trustworthy manner." Trust requires consistent commitment to integrity and purity. Trust takes time to build and requires intentionality and purposefulness. On the other hand, trust can be easily and quickly broken.

What does it mean to be a trustworthy person and to contribute toward building trust in marriage? Trustworthiness requires deliberately thinking through decisions and understanding the ramifications and results. A trustworthy spouse wants the other spouse to be able to have confidence and does not want to harm or disappoint in any way. This is proven by consistently choosing actions that strengthen the trust in the relationship.

A Spiritual and Moral Compass

It is easy to trust a person who has a strong spiritual and moral compass in life. Such a person acts in ways that honor God and show love for other people appropriately. Having the right priorities in life shows trustworthiness. Intentionally acting with kindness and respect toward others, specifically the spouse, builds trustworthiness and predictability. This brings assurance to the marriage. Such dependability instills strength and peace in a marriage.

> "Love the Lord your God with all your heart and with all your soul and with all your mind and with all your strength." The second is this: "Love your neighbor as yourself." There is no commandment greater than these. (Mark 12:30–31)

True worship means obeying and honoring God. We worship what our heart loves. The greatest joys flow from an obedient and thankful heart toward God. When one loves the Lord first and most, love also overflows to others. Joyfully serving and sacrificing for those God has given us to love and care for maintains the trust they deserve.

Melissa and Gregory are members of a church and are involved in a small group. However, on Sundays Melissa has to be the one who wakes up the family, fixes breakfast, and gets the children ready. Gregory is often the last one up and the slowest to get ready. Melissa feels as if she has an extra child and longs for Gregory to be the family leader who is excited about worship.

The desire to maintain the quality of the relationship instead of satisfying personal agendas brings lasting benefits. This results in relationship reliability and is accompanied with joy and confidence. A spiritual compass is based on following Jesus Christ as Lord and obeying the truths in the Bible. It leads to a moral compass of integrity, purity, honesty, and respectability.

God is the highest and final authority for life. The commitment to obey God requires a life lived with the desire to apply biblical truth. God has established principles and guidelines for life, actions, and relationships. These teachings of truth are in the Bible. We cannot in our human perspective have wisdom or understanding to establish what is spiritually true or morally correct. We must have a biblical understanding and application.

A spiritual compass then determines a moral compass and results in a godly person who keeps promises, has integrity, and is trustworthy. That person knows right from wrong based on God's Word and consistently chooses what is right. A person who honors God and others is dependable and steadfast. This takes away uncertainty and replaces it with confidence in the relationship.

A person can be trusted when a strong moral and biblical focus governs his or her life. In marriage, when a person has a heart that seeks after the Lord and reflects the character of Jesus Christ, the spouse feels remarkable peace. It is easy to trust a person who loves God and acts with conviction in everything he or she does. This conviction is from God's Word and not only personal opinion.

Trustworthiness is exhibited by keeping promises and being honest, righteous, and holy. A person of integrity does the right thing even when no one else is watching and even when it is difficult, costly, or inconvenient. Such people have a strong reputation of trustworthiness. They live to honor God, value life, and treat others in respectful ways. Trustworthiness means doing what one says and following through with accountability and dependability. This binds hearts and minds together.

> Trust in the Lord with all your heart
>   and lean not on your own understanding;
> in all your ways acknowledge Him,
>   and He will make your paths straight.
> (Proverbs 3:5–6)

But just as he who called you is holy, so be holy in
all you do; for it is written: "Be holy, because I am
holy." (1 Peter 1:15–16)

Sacrificial Love

Trust is the confidence that a spouse will act in love. Love is
shown in actions taken in another's best interest. It is easy to trust
a person who places the spouse and family members as priorities
and shows sacrificial love toward them. This love is exhibited by
putting others' needs and desires above personal desires. This
is shown through serving, kindness, consideration, honor, and
respect. It is most meaningful when each spouse has sacrificial
love.

Assurance is felt when a spouse knows that his or her needs,
interests, and desires will be held in high regard. It feels safe when
one is treated with predictable, steadfast love. Love focuses on
what is respectful and positive for others. Manipulating to achieve
personal desires and agendas is the opposite of love. Don't let
personal hobbies and interests become too important. Give priority
toward your spouse and your marriage. True love is sacrificial and
selfless.

> … not looking to your own interests but each
> of you to the interests of the others. In your
> relationships with one another, have the same
> mindset as Christ Jesus. (Philippians 2:4–5)

This passage says that Jesus Christ modeled the ultimate act of
sacrificial love. He willingly laid down His life for the forgiveness
of sins and the gift of eternal life for all who would believe in Him.
Selfless love is evidenced through serving, benefiting others, and
treating them with love and respect. It includes striving to honor

others and helping lighten another's load. Sacrificial love is the hallmark of a life surrendered to Jesus Christ. It strengthens a marriage when each spouse is looking for ways to show love for each other instead of self.

Takes Care of Responsibilities

Trust grows in a marriage when a spouse is careful to be attentive to his or her responsibilities. The commitment to follow up with chores at home, take care of things that need to be done, and be motivated to stay current with repairs and maintenance gives a sense of devotion to and love for family members. Having a positive attitude about tasks and being proactive to address responsibilities without needing to be reminded show the proper priorities.

Following through on commitments brings a sense of being valued. Good intentions are not the same as disciplined follow-through on needed actions. Being diligent and motivated is respectful to others. Staying up with responsibilities builds trust in the marriage. Listen to your spouse's assessments of anything that needs to be done, and take care of it as soon as possible. This will proclaim your love for your spouse. The result will be trust building.

Chores and responsibilities are a part of life. An attitude of accepting responsibilities with a willing and positive response goes a long way in building confidence and trust in the marriage relationship. This is the opposite of avoidance, becoming easily frustrated, acting like it is an imposition or a drudgery, procrastinating, or doing a sloppy job. If your spouse has concerns about needed repairs, examine your own life to see how responsive you are to the expressed needs and desires. Perhaps procrastination is the main issue, not the request for help.

Gene and Leslie have purchased a house forty years old with many needed repairs. It was a great buy, and both said they were willing to make the necessary updates. Since then, Gene seems uninterested and unmotivated. He is not responsive when she asks him to fix something. Now the leaks and chipped paint loom large. Leslie's trust in Gene has eroded, and she feels disregarded.

> If a man is lazy, the rafters sag;
>> if his hands are idle, the house leaks.
> (Ecclesiastes 10:18)

> You, my brothers, were called to be free. But do not use your freedom to indulge the sinful nature; rather, serve one another in love. (Galatians 5:13)

Exhibits Self Control

When spiritual and emotional maturity is evident in a person's life, it builds trust in the relationship. These characteristics are seen in self-control and produce feelings of emotional safety. A life that is out of control harms others and breaks trust. This results in emotional chaos and devastated relationships. Meaningful self-control is evidenced in all areas of life. Some of these include appropriately controlling emotions, spending patterns, time schedules and actions.

Emotionally

A person is a trust builder when he or she speaks calmly, treats others lovingly, and exhibits self-control even when upset. Anyone can express feelings reactively with disregard for others. It requires maturity and discipline to dissipate intense emotions and choose to respond in a measured and controlled way. Love means acting in a loving, calm, and respectful way even when one is upset.

Cory and Danielle feel dishonored by each other. Their pattern of communicating has become increasingly impatient, angry, and volatile. They each feel justified and misunderstood. They need to seek biblical counsel, be willing to acknowledge personal sin, and confess and replace the destructive reactions with healthy responses. They need someone to give them hope and help for change.

Unbridled anger is sinful and destroys trust. Anger is very destructive in relationships. It discourages, crushes, and disrespects others. It leaves vast devastation in the hearts and lives of a spouse and/or family members. Selfish anger is quick and destructive. However, it takes a long time to heal the emotional pain caused by sinful anger.

> A fool gives full vent to his anger,
>> but a wise man keeps himself under control.
>> (Proverbs 29:11)

> But the fruit of the Spirit is love, joy, peace, patience, kindness, goodness, faithfulness, gentleness and self-control. (Galatians 5:22–23)

The Holy Spirit indwells Christians. These characteristics are the result or the fruit of the Spirit abiding in believers. They are relational words and are evidenced in interaction with others. Since these qualities are from the Holy Spirit, they are not the normal first human emotional response. They are usually the opposite of what we might normally want to do. Exhibiting the fruit of the Holy Spirit means surrendering to God and letting Him control how we express our emotions, regardless of the circumstances.

To replace normal human reactions with characteristics produced by the Holy Spirit is to let God have control of our hearts and to die to self. Instead of acting according to human feelings and desires, there is a commitment to pause and choose to act in a calm and godly way. This is hard to do when emotions come fast and intensely. However, it pays rich dividends relationally when the right commitments develop into loving habits.

Sexually

Boundaries are discussed in detail in chapter 13. However, one area of self-control involves how spouses interact with every other relationship. The marriage is the priority relationship above all others. A married couple builds trust when each spouse handles the marital relationship as the most treasured relationship. Actions with every other relationship should be respectful toward the spouse even if the spouse is not present. Acting with proper protection of the marriage builds trust and confidence.

There must be unwavering promises for sexual purity in the marriage. Compromises or indiscretions should not occur. Husbands and wives build trust in their marriage when they commit to behaving appropriately around other people. Both spouses need to be clearly committed to respect each other in every outside relationship. Nothing should ever make a spouse feel uncomfortable.

A husband honors his wife by not looking at other women or at inappropriate images, whether on billboards, TV, movies, or electronic media. There should be a commitment to look away without lingering. A wise and godly person understands that what one looks at greatly impacts the heart. For a husband to think that looking at other women and images is harmless and acceptable is selfish and reckless. It is disrespectful toward the wife.

> I made a covenant with my eyes
>> not to look lustfully at a young woman.
> (Job 31:1)

> Above all else, guard your heart,
>> for it is the wellspring of life. (Proverbs 4:23)

A wife honors her husband by dressing with discretion and handling herself with propriety in relating to others. Nothing about a woman should give the appearance that she is trying to gain the attention of other men. There is a strong unspoken message that says, *I've been chosen, and I belong to someone*, when a woman dresses in a pretty way, with modesty. Her love for the Lord and love for her husband can be seen in her smile and radiance if her clothing doesn't draw the attention in other ways.

Time Commitments

> Be very careful, then, how you live—not as unwise
> but as wise ... (Ephesians 5:15)

The way a person keeps commitments reveals a lot about one's character and love for his or her spouse. When marriage partners make agreements about their time schedules, activities, and priorities, they should be highly motivated to be accountable in those areas. Marriage spouses are trustworthy when they are dependable about being where they say they would be and doing what they said they would do. Openness and truthfulness about calendars and commitments build trust and reliability.

When there is a willingness to show schedules, discuss plans, and update as changes occur, then a spouse can feel that the partner wants to keep them informed. Talk with your spouse before you schedule any events with anyone outside of work. As spouses, stay current with each other about events, whereabouts, and time commitments, confidence and trust grow. Be fully honest and always open to discuss all activities. This shows faithfulness in what you say and do. Additionally, it provides a safety factor for each of you as you keep each other informed throughout the day.

Finances

Other examples of trust-building self-control include keeping commitments about finances and resources. Discussing finances together builds a sense of being a team in the marriage. Frequent updates on expenses, purchases, paying bills, and savings are all important. Disregarding agreements, hiding things, or being irresponsible in finances will quickly bring concern and break the trust in the marriage. It takes a long time to rebuild the trust.

Work together with finances, goals, and decisions. Talk about finances regularly and completely. Love your spouse more than money, and treat your spouse with respect and consideration as your equal partner in all areas of finances. Be responsive to each other's concerns and ideas. Make decisions together, and keep the agreements you make.

Moves toward the Marriage with Commitment and Love

Marriages are growing and not static. Either a marriage is growing stronger and more delightful, or it is weakening and becoming more distant. Through the course of a marriage the sense of closeness may fluctuate a little, but it should be growing and becoming more fulfilling. Healthy marriages work on issues and continue to grow closer together. Unhealthy marriages continue to struggle unless they learn how to apply positive commitments and actions.

Some factors that diminish and harm the trust in marriages can be directly linked to emotional neglect in the marriage, complacency, lack of consistency, taking each other for granted, disrespect, selfishness, negative attitudes, lying, laziness, and minimizing spousal concerns. When these creep into a marriage, the couple must seek help in order to turn the marriage around.

Marriages can change and improve. It requires insight to recognize areas that are lacking and the desire and willingness to improve in those areas. That is one of the specific benefits of marital counseling. A biblically trained counselor can help marriage partners recognize areas of needed growth and provide the methods and steps that can be beneficial and positive.

The spouses need to put forth the effort to grow stronger. As a couple is open to explore areas of problems or needed growth, changes begin to happen. The resulting emotional satisfaction helps motivate the couple for further growth. It is a joy to see things improving in a marriage. This can produce more energy and desire for attacking the tougher issues with success.

Investment for marital growth can produce more happiness and a sense of accomplishment. Feelings of increased relational closeness are very invigorating in a marriage. As a marriage becomes stronger, time together for the spouses becomes more meaningful and enjoyable. This encourages commitment to resolve issues and communicate more effectively. Each new step of growth results in increased hope and feelings of affection.

Joshua and Chelsea have been married for six years and have two young children. They feel as though the happiness and trust are mediocre in their marriage. Joshua spends a lot of time on his phone and computer. Chelsea sometimes spends above their agreed limits and isn't always open about her expenditures. Joshua explodes in anger, and Chelsea is not always reliable in what she says. Both say they want a better marriage, want to resolve conflicts, want to be trustworthy, and are willing to take steps to grow and change.

They need hope and guidance to improve their marriage. The good news is that it is very possible if they will seek help from an objective, godly person who will help them address issues and make necessary changes. They need to evaluate strengths and weaknesses in their marriage, apply biblical guidelines, and move forward with positive steps. With God's help and their willingness, their marriage can be radically transformed and changed into a loving and trusting marriage.

Trust is built and strengthened in a marriage when each partner is confident that the spouse will consistently do the right thing in all situations. That includes keeping promises, acting with integrity, handling emotions with restraint, being unselfish, honoring appropriate boundaries regarding people outside the marriage, and being responsible and diligent to be trustworthy.

God will guide and comfort each person who seeks Him regarding these very important issues. Trust in the Lord. He holds the puzzle box top. Jesus Christ knows the big picture, sees everything, and will help you know how to put the pieces together. God responds to each person with His love, righteousness, and grace. His comfort and help are abounding and steadfast. He loves with an infinite love and cares about every detail of your experiences and feelings.

Trust in marriage is of great worth. It is not overrated. Trust is worth strengthening and restoring. You are worth it. Your marriage is worth it. Certainly, your relationship with the Lord is worth the commitment to have a marriage with a beautiful and strong trust that honors Him. Commit to be a trust builder in your marriage. Experience marriage as God designed it and His blessings for years to come.

Endnotes

1   Larson & Olson (2010) Prepare/Enrich Life Innovations. Used with permission.

2   Northwestern Mutual, "Planning and Progress Study 2013" and "Planning and Progress Study 2014" Used with permission by Preaching Today. Copyright 2015. Original illustration can be accessed here: http://www.preachingtoday.com/illustrations/2015/february/2020915.html.

Printed in the United States
By Bookmasters